NIGHTWATCH
An Inquiry Into Solitude

NIGHTWATCH
An Inquiry Into Solitude

*Alone on the Prairie
with the Hutterites*

Robert Rhodes

Good Books
Intercourse, PA 17534
800/762-7171
www.GoodBooks.com

A Note About the Text

Because the Hutterites, like the members of many plain groups, prefer to remain relatively anonymous, some effort, though not much, has been made to maintain the privacy of certain people in this narrative. This includes both Hutterite and non-Hutterite figures in this book, but only extends to the changing of a few names. All places and events in this book exist and took place to the best of the author's recollection.

Acknowledgments

Quotations attributed to *The Chronicle of The Hutterian Brethren* are from these two publications:
- *The Chronicle of the Hutterian Brethren, Volume I.* Rifton, NY: Plough Publishing House, 1987.
- *The Chronicle of the Hutterian Brethren, Volume II.* Ste. Agathe, MB: Crystal Spring Colony, 1998.

Cover photograph by Jan Gleysteen
Design by Cliff Snyder

NIGHTWATCH

Copyright © 2009 by Good Books, Intercourse, PA 17534
International Standard Book Number: 978-1-56148-666-3

Library of Congress Catalog Card Number: 2009017181

Library of Congress Cataloging-in-Publication Data

Rhodes, Robert E., 1964-
Nightwatch : an inquiry into solitude : alone on the prairie with the Hutterites / Robert Rhodes.
    p. cm.
ISBN 978-1-56148-666-3 (pbk. : alk. paper) 1. Hutterian Brethren. 2. Hutterian Brethren--Minnesota--Gibbon. 3. Christian communities--Minnesota--Gibbon. 4. Gibbon (Minn.)--Church history. I. Title.
BX8129.H8R46 2009
289.7'3--dc22   2009017181

For Duann, who also lived this way.

Have you had sight of Me, Jonas My child?
Mercy within mercy within mercy.

    – Thomas Merton, "Fire Watch, July 4, 1952,"
      The Sign of Jonas.

chapter
ONE

***Nightwatch, Starland Colony, Gibbon, Minnesota,
December 1999.***

*At night, back when I was a communist, the place where we
lived on the prairie of southern Minnesota took up a cloak of
indivisible silence. In winter, this quiet was disrupted only by
the wind. Because it seemed to last for months at a time, these
gales that blew down from Canada and Lake Superior became
another dimension of the same vast absence of sound.*

*But whenever the wind stopped, all perception was instantly
restored – the creaking of a metal sign, the mailbox vibrating
on its jittery post after someone tossed in a letter and slammed
the hatch. Everything alive seemed to pause with the wind,
listening to its sudden departure and puzzling over whether
some vague disaster were about to strike.*

Starland Colony, a community of the Hutterian Brethren —
a Christian peace church that has been living in large farming
communes for nearly 500 years, from eastern Europe to the
plains of the United States and Canada — occupies about 2,000
acres in extreme northwest Sibley County. Within a short walk
of the main community, with its houses, barns, a large communal kitchen, and a state-of-the-art metal working shop, were
the bounds of two other counties, Renville and McLeod. These
coincided a mile or two from our long, narrow section road. All
told, we occupied a very small, distinctly confined corner of
what most people would charitably call "nowhere."

Our tiny mail town, Gibbon, was seven miles of right angles
to our south and west. A locus of bars and a VFW hall and a
large, imposing grain elevator, Gibbon is perhaps best known
for a rambling klatch of buildings known as the Gibbon Ballroom. Each broad, low structure in the 12-acre compound had
its own name — prominent among them the Boom Room and
the Pumpernickel Room (noted for its frosty air-conditioning).
There, each July the town hosted a long, perhaps mildly lost,
weekend of beer and sausages and three-step dance music
known as Polka Days. This revel was attended by hundreds of
RV-driving cloggers from across the Great Plains, all dressed in
costumes of bright, quarrelsome colors. One summer, a sign on
one of the RVs, during a year when the future of Polka Days
seemed in question, expressed the neighborly resignation of
towns like this: "Old friends never die. They just polka away."
So it would be in Gibbon.

Each year, while the staid and plain-dressed Hutterites
stood a resolute watch from only a few miles away, bands such
as Chuck Thiel and the Jolly Ramblers, Ray Sands and the

Polka Dots, and Becky and the Ivanhoe Dutchmen held court here.

This night, though, on the marquee outside the Boom Room, rocking tenuously in the steady northerly wind of December, the motto of Gibbon's most popular establishment summed up the festival's, and the town's, prevailing rationale: "Stay Young, Go Dancing." Underneath was a bitter footnote written by economics and the ice that often encased this land for nearly half the year: "Closed for the Season."

Gibbon, it seemed, was a place where many diverse worlds crossed paths. In November 1997, during a four-day blizzard, the popular Minnesota radio show *A Prairie Home Companion* broadcast from the Ballroom, bringing all sorts of other strange-looking people to gawk at this faraway expanse of sky. The well-heeled appearance of these SUV-driving city people only reminded us locals of how austere, and of how separate, we all really were. One snowbound morning before the show aired, when I had gone to the Gibbon post office, I saw the program's host, Garrison Keillor, emerging from Thorson's Bakery across the street. The first time I'd seen Thorson's, I'd thought it sounded like one of the hangouts in Keillor's quasi-fictional Lake Wobegon, Minnesota. In downtown Gibbon — the glittering, snowy glare bouncing off the grain elevator — here was life reflecting someone's vision of art.

Due east of Gibbon, down a straight, well-traveled highway, was a slightly larger town, Winthrop. Despite having no ballroom, or even very many bars, Winthrop seemed to be surviving slightly better than Gibbon.

The houses in Winthrop were orderly, and a public library actually seemed to thrive, despite the preponderance of well-read Westerns and romance novels. Even if they were not great literature, these were a fluffy intellectual staple for many on the lonely, snowy plains, where wind-ravaged hearts and minds either turned inward every winter, or drew people to congregate in the Legion Hall over languorous glasses of Grain Belt beer.

Winthrop also had a nursing home, where many of the women from the Hutterite colony went to help with sewing several times a month. This was where the old corn farmers and their sturdy, hard-working wives — finally forsaking land and crops and solitude for life in "town" — went to spend their fading dotage or to wait out whatever fatal illnesses would strike them down.

In the middle distance, down the highway that led eventually to Mankato and Rochester, flowed the steady plume of steam from a corn-fed ethanol plant, the only sign of substantial industry other than field crops for miles around.

To the north of Starland, on a razor-straight county road, was a pinpoint on the map known as Fernando, ubiquitous in its handful of white clapboard houses and an old Lutheran church, the slender steeple of which could be seen for several miles, surrounded by a stand of cottonwood trees.

Fernando, at some point, must have been terribly important to the local population because the nearest highway curves more than two miles out of its way to pass through there. Still, all but a few have moved away, and a tiny store where the colony children used to ride their bikes to buy ice cream on summer afternoons has long since closed.

Passing through this wide spot in the road, which one had to do to travel north from the community, we used to joke on the farm radio about entering the "greater Fernando metroplex" and the hostile risks of "central Fernando" late at night.

There was not much else to joke about in such pristine isolation, so we made do.

North of Fernando was the place we usually referred to when we spoke of going to "town." Hutchinson, the seat of McLeod County, had about 20,000 people and a regional hospital where most of the colony children were born, including two of our own. Every day, several trips from the colony, using one of the community's several minivans or pickup trucks, would be made to Hutchinson. Medical appointments, assorted orthodontia, minor business needs, fishing, or just a need to escape the sometimes cramped routine of Hutterian existence for a few hours – all sorts of things called us, Siren-like, to Hutchinson.

Similar poles of attraction lay to our south, at New Ulm – a scenic German-themed town set in a valley along the flood-prone Minnesota River – and Mankato, a city of about 50,000 southeast of New Ulm across more rolling, tillable prairie. Two other Hutterite colonies, Neuhof and Elmendorf, which emerged from various colonies in South Dakota, lay outside the small town of Mountain Lake, a historically Mennonite town near the Iowa border.

To the east, about 80 miles away, lay the greatest attraction of all. Minneapolis and St. Paul blinked and hummed with life of an entirely different speed and dimension. Deep in the night, the red beacons of passenger jets on their final approach to the Minneapolis airport could be seen gliding above us in a steady, almost soundless stream. Some nights, they flew so low that the faint thunder of their turbines could be heard as their broad wings slashed at the thin, cold air.

Elsewhere, in the gently rolling prairie that was our universe, was total emptiness, field after field where feed corn, soybeans, sugar beets, sweet peas, and alfalfa grew in spring and turned our summers into a lush paradise.

A few farmers — nearly all of whom had town jobs to supplement the income from their 500-acre spreads — gambled with winter wheat. But the unpredictability of the snows — sometimes coming by Halloween and lingering until mid-April — made this a difficult proposition.

If the deep snow was not proof enough, the mailboxes along the main road reminded us this was Minnesota, with Norse and Germanic surnames — Bjorklund, Stark, Renner, Klukas, Jaeger, Fischer. These stood at the head of short drives leading to muddy dairies and hog farms, all arrayed in the landlocked precision of farms everywhere.

But this night, a few days before Christmas, the entire world was frozen, knee-deep in snow with a brutal, windblown cold that could keep the air far below zero for weeks at a time. By 10 p.m., the 120 people who lived in Starland Colony, in this "town" set apart from all the others by centuries of tradition and tenacious faith, were going to bed. All except for the night watchman, whose unthanked, often dismally lonesome duties had fallen to me on this brilliant, frozen, starlit evening.

Stepping into the steady wind, I was bundled in a bulky denim barn coat that my wife said made me resemble a hobo — while I preferred to believe I resembled a convict, belonging to what some of our friends deemed a religious Alcatraz. I picked my way across the packed snow to the watchman's truck, a small blue Ford left in front of my house by the previous night's protector. This came along with a flashlight that was the watchman's badge, and a set of keys that would open nearly every door on the place. Not that very many doors were kept locked. In fact, it was just the opposite.

This night, it was nearly 20 below zero but the truck started right away as I felt my beard and nostrils thaw in the slight shelter of the cab.

~

Aside from a few lights in some of the houses, and the scattering of tall tungsten lamps wobbling in the wind near some of the main buildings, the entire community had fallen into shadow. Even the 70-foot leg on the community's feed mill, once festooned with a large blue star during Christmas until a spring tornado blew it cartwheeling away, seemed to recede into the total, absorbing darkness.

As I drove away from our house and toward the long, narrow metal shop, where our lives and livelihoods were mostly centered, the watch had begun.

chapter
TWO

The place where I grew up, and where my life's inquiry into loneliness and solitude began, lay in a long, broad hip of the Mississippi River in northeastern Arkansas. Wilson, in Mississippi County, was about 30 miles from the Missouri Bootheel. Our town came up adjacent to Island No. 35, a large cutoff formed in part by the devastating New Madrid earthquakes of 1811-12. These quakes changed the course of the Mississippi in numerous places and sent sandblows, small volcanoes of liquefacted silt, spewing all over that stretch of the Delta.

New Madrid, Missouri, which was then part of the Louisiana Territory, was the general locus for the series of strong quakes, which began in December 1811 and continued through February 7, 1812, when the greatest jolt of all fell like some divine sledgehammer. According to legend passed off as historic certainty, the big quake rang church bells in Boston and cracked sidewalks in Washington, D.C., both of which seem rather fanciful.

Nonetheless, the apocalyptic effect of the quakes on the local region, and on the entire middle Mississippi and Ohio Valley regions, is well established. In northwestern Tennessee, a massive shift in the terrain caused the Mississippi to flow backwards for a time and fill in present-day Reelfoot Lake.

On the shores of Reelfoot, seismograms still detect constant tremors, most so faint they cannot be felt on the surface. Other tremors, though, none of which has exceeded 5.2 on the Richter scale since the 1812 quake, deliver a significant shock, reminding everyone that a major fault system fractures the Earth below their feet.

The New Madrid Fault is said to run far beneath the surface from just outside Marked Tree, Arkansas, to far southern Illinois. Along its length, small quakes and temblors have bloomed throughout modern times, bringing a growing concern that another big shock would deal a tottering death blow to large cities such as Memphis and St. Louis. Living under such a threat, though it seldom sprang to mind except when another tremor struck, only enhanced the sense of isolation I felt as a child.

Visible evidence of the historic quakes could be found only a short distance from the house where I grew up, in a place that played a big part in my childhood. There, along the deep curve of Dean's Island, a large peninsula that juts into the main channel of the Mississippi, the river's ancient bed was still visible. It was amid the oxbows and diversion channels that I went fishing nearly every day of my life, from the time I was eight or nine until I was nearly 14.

In a culture that essentially had no middle class – only an upper strata and a desperately low-income labor and sharecropper society – our family was quite well off. My two younger brothers and I attended private schools in West Memphis, Arkansas, and Memphis, Tennessee. We were members of hereditary organizations such as the Children of the Confederacy, a rather patrician group that took as members the descendants of those who fought for the South in the Civil War. We drove around in broad, overweight Chryslers and Cadillacs with little thought for the fuel they consumed or the pollution they belched into the environment.

My father, Bentley Rhodes, the son of a millionaire lumber baron from south Arkansas, owned an insurance company and traded stocks and bonds, as well as owning some lucrative farmland. Because our family was well provided for and I went to parochial school away from Wilson, we were relatively remote as children. This especially was the case for me, not only because I had virtually no friends my age in town, but because of my strange and often annoying intellectual curiosity, which erected walls even harder to breach than those built by money or life's other unfair circumstances.

We also had servants in our home. At various times, these "housekeepers" or "maids," as polite society called them, did all our cooking and cleaning and helped look after us children. The woman who worked for us the longest was Josephine Polk, an older black woman. Josephine had lived much of her life about two miles north of Wilson off Highway 61 in a red tar-paper house with holes in the floor. Though too large to be thought of as a shack, that was what it was.

Josephine was a short, round woman who, like many of her generation, resembled a living stereotype, with tightly-braided pigtails and a dark, pressed bandanna wrapped around her forehead. She did not read, nor could she write. If she ever completed more than a year or two of grade school, which would have been sometime in the 1920s, I never heard her speak of it and I certainly never asked, having been taught that such intimate, much less interracial, inquiry was rude.

Josephine came to us in a rather serendipitous manner. When my father saw her walking to another family's house some distance from town one morning in the summer heat, he stopped his car and told Josephine to get in. In his usual manner, he got down to business straight away.

"If you'll come and take care of my boys and my house, I'll come get you and take you home again at night."

They also discussed some matter of pay, which apparently was more than Josie was getting on her present job. It was paid in cash, too, so as not to interfere with the welfare checks and food stamps that kept the many children and grandchildren she supported from the virtual certainty of starvation, or at least malnutrition.

According to the story, Josephine was not quick to accept my father's offer, and for good reason. Our reputation as roughnecks and undisciplined rogues, even at such a young age, was well known.

"Mr. Bentley, I've heard about those boys of yours," she told my father, speaking not only of my younger brothers and me, but of four older brothers, including one who had Down syndrome and lived in what was then still called an institution. All of this older crop of boys had wreaked their share of havoc as well.

Still, she came to stay with us the very next day and was part of our family for a good many years. My father usually went to fetch Josephine about 6:30 in the morning, and my mother would take her home around 5:30 p.m. Driving down the long dirt road to Josephine's house, surrounded by cotton fields and with a small white church almost directly across the road from the stand of trees that offered her house its only shelter from the heat, I always felt ashamed.

Riding in our shiny green and white Cadillac with the electric windows and door locks and leather upholstered seats that were far better than anything Josephine owned, I believed even as a child that I was committing a grave offense. Showing ourselves, parading down one of the poorest roads in Mississippi County, was a terrible affront, I felt, and I could hardly bear not to hide myself in the back seat, where Josephine's family and neighbors couldn't see me, even though they knew I was there and would welcome me with strong, lingering hugs whenever we arrived.

Only once did I go into Josephine's house. The gaps in the old cypress flooring revealed the house's dark, fetid underside where dogs and cats ran and ancient weeds and tree roots were bleached ghostly white by the shifting darkness. The furniture was threadbare and seemed to double as beds for some of the dozen or so adults and children sheltered there each night. In her crisp, starched maid's uniform, which fit her like a snug nurse's smock, Josephine looked like a visitor in this place herself, someone sent from afar to establish order. But she was the matriarch of all there was to see, the illiterate woman who earned money to feed the hungry mouths and who never seemed to complain about her lot in life.

Though I did not think she could read, I would see her occasionally thumbing through an old black Bible, which she spread out on her soft and substantial lap. Even if she could not make out the words, she obviously gained something from the book she held in her strong, rough hands. She never quoted the Bible to us when we were children, but she was a church-going woman and would brook no unrighteousness from any of us, in language or deed. She did not smoke or drink, and never swore that I heard, though these practices were well-known – especially smoking and swearing – among the adults in our house.

She also maintained, in the most natural way possible, the required decorum that arrangements like ours called for in the South. From the time I was seven years old until I left home and never saw her again, Josephine always addressed me, no matter the situation, as "Mr. Bob." My father, her benefactor and defender whenever conflict arose, was "Mr. Bentley." But my mother, her critic and taskmaster, was always "Ms. Rhodes" and "Ma'am."

Because I had two younger brothers, I was not entirely without companionship, but even in my choice of friends I was quite eccentric. Around the time I was nine, I became friends with Aurora Finn, a girl my age who lived nearby and who enjoyed fishing as much as I did. In time, we became inseparable. The fact that we were of opposite genders never entered into our calculations at that age. We were friends, and we shared a childhood as oddly idyllic as it was sometimes lonely.

My mother, Betty, had been a child prodigy on classical piano and organ, performing in public at a very young age in Chicago. Crimson-haired and slim as a girl, photographs of her show a serious youngster seated at the keyboard. As an adult, she was quite accomplished, playing in several churches over the years. Unfortunately, because of her rather broad intellectual interests, she often found herself bored and frustrated living in such a small town. Observing her in daily life was a study in loneliness, tempered only at times by the odd musical distraction. Working with my father in his rather hectic and, at times, high-stakes insurance business was not fulfilling, either.

My mother was most herself when she was performing, with or without an audience, and so our home was often filled with classical music. The 20th century organ works of Olivier Messiaen, along with the Baroque classics of Bach, were her *forte*. The large Hammond concert organ we had in our house, in a soundproof room specially constructed to accommodate it, could be heard down the street if a window were left open. In addition to Sunday church services, my mother also played at weddings and funerals. And I recall several occasions when professional musicians from Memphis, lured by tales of a top-drawer organ hidden away in this remote river town, appeared at our door at strange hours, usually brought by someone who had visited before. More than once, my mother, dressed in her nightclothes, ran the instrument through its paces in some impromptu recital. Still, this was not enough for her.

My mother was desperately bored and, in many ways, would remain so for the rest of her life. Aside from hymns and her classical repertoire, the only other music I heard her express appreciation for was that of the Beatles, which she simply said was "put together rather well." She told me once that when she had seen the Beatles on the Ed Sullivan Show in 1964, a few weeks after I was born, she had become smitten with Paul McCartney. I always thought this said a lot about the deeply musical person who raised me.

To my dismay, Mother was not overly fond of Aurora, thinking her too much of a tomboy. (My father teasingly called her "Huck," which Aurora politely disliked). To me, this did not matter. When my mother criticized Aurora because of her appearance or the tattered jeans or cowboy boots she favored, I always defended her.

"Please don't say that, Mother," I pleaded when I was 11 or 12, afraid her remarks would wound my closest friend. Aurora was bright and pleasant and outgoing, the total opposite of the taciturn, sometimes profane brood I was part of. At times, my defenses of Aurora surprised and confused even me. "I think she's beautiful," I told my mother more than once.

All I knew was that I felt empty and alone when I did not see her, and that the days we spent together, wandering the woods and waterways of our isolated part of the world, meant everything to me.

Aurora was the only person who almost never heard the debilitating stutter I developed in early grade school – a vocal perplexity that drove me even further inward. For some reason, I never stuttered when I was alone with Aurora. With others, however, especially in school or among my family, I spoke with great fear and reticence. Because of this, I still don't like to speak on the telephone, though my stammer gradually disappeared in my teens, reviving only rarely now.

My life would undergo a sudden and injurious change one afternoon in August 1977, when I was 13 years old. It would be a turn of events that probably had as much to do with the future course of my life, including our encounter with the Hutterites, as anything else. I often have wondered what course my life might have taken if it had not been so suddenly and violently derailed. I certainly doubt I would have arrived at the same ideals, or gained the spiritual curiosity that eventually led us to the colony if I had not spent several years laid up and isolated by these unforeseen developments.

Like many sudden changes of course in life, something weird and nearly ridiculous had its role to play. In this case, it was Elvis Presley. Because of the rock 'n' roll icon's sudden death in Memphis the week before, my mother, brothers, and I had gone up to southeastern Missouri on the Saturday afternoon when Presley's funeral was to be held. Usually, we did our grocery shopping in Memphis on Saturday, not far in fact from the Graceland mansion, which until Elvis' death was in a relatively quiet part of town. But because of the heat and chaos and crowds that had taken over the city, we decided instead to visit my maternal grandmother overnight in the small town of Chaffee, Missouri, where my mother and her sister and brother had been born and grew up and where my uncle still lived.

Early that morning, before we left, I had gone on my daily bike ride, typically a 25-mile run that took me from our house all the way to the Mississippi at San Souci Landing, an industrial port about 12 miles to the north. These bicycle rides, though I could not articulate it at the time, were periods I would spend in a kind of deep meditation. Because the landscape around me was so empty and flat, my attention usually turned inward with the miles. I nearly always rode out of town through several miles of cultivated farmland seeded with cotton or soybeans. First I went past a small settlement, really just a gathering of pleasant, shaded houses, known as Carson Lake, where a family named Cullom lived.

Then I rode a meandering path beyond an abandoned cotton gin to another town called Driver, where the Lowrance Bros. plantation was headquartered, and finally up Highway

61 toward the county seat, Osceola, which had a large bronze-domed courthouse like many Southern county seats. Although most of my route was smooth and paved, there was a significant levee to climb just before reaching the port complex, which had a shady park where you could watch the tugs propel the barges laden with soybeans from the sprawling Bunge International processing plant. Next to Bunge, also on the river, was a Union Carbide graphite factory.

When I got back home about 10 a.m. that day, just as the stifling August heat was beginning to shriek and swelter, I did not know that I would never ride a bicycle again. Shortly after dinner, we drove to Chaffee, a railroad town about two hours from Wilson and 90 miles south of St. Louis. That afternoon, my uncle, Tom Davenport, and I went to throw a Frisbee around the backyard before supper. With the heat still at full smolder and lightning bugs starting to flicker in the honeysuckle, I made a running, flying leap to pull down a wild throw. During the next three or four seconds, the course of my life changed forever, in ways I still cannot always comprehend.

Landing hard at a sharply broken angle, my right knee and lower leg shattered, leaving me with a compound fracture and a knee not only crushed but shredded of most of its soft tissue. My uncle lifted me into the back of my mother's Coupe de Ville, which was broad enough for me to stretch out to nearly full length, and rushed me to the hospital in Cape Girardeau, about 20 miles away. I scarcely remember the trip other than the horrid jolts whenever we crossed railroad tracks. My skin became cold and pale as I went into shock, enduring the most intense and indescribable pain of my life.

At the hospital, I remember my uncle running into the ER to get a nurse before I evidently passed out. Meanwhile, the doctors twisted and set my leg back into shape and dosed me with an exuberant amount of morphine that kept me in kind of an ecstatic, slightly nauseated fog for the next few days. Two days later, on Monday, I was still hovering in semi-shock when I was taken to the main Methodist Hospital on Union Avenue in Memphis, a place that would become a second home for me in the years to come.

After I was seen by an orthopedist, and had preliminary repairs conducted and my right leg encased in a massive cast that ran from my hip to my big toe, I set out on a course of further operations, excruciating bouts of rehabilitation, and seemingly endless hospital stays that would dominate my life for the next five years. When I wasn't in the hospital, I was either confined to bed at home or occupying a wheelchair at school. By the time I was 18, I had probably spent a solid four or five months in three hospitals in Memphis, and despite all the medical attention I received, was still told I would never walk normally, if at all. During all this, because of the injuries to my knee, my back began to deteriorate as well, causing even more pain and further impeding my progress.

At first, I accepted this, because it seemed that even though I was a young and relatively strong person, I had sustained an injury I could neither understand nor overcome. The glowering cracks and bulges on the X-rays revealed only destruction, and my withered, unmoving leg showed little of the wherewithal it would need to function properly. In those days, most orthopedic procedures were still conducted with considerable trauma to the body, not like today when arthroscopic surgery makes many procedures outpatient and greatly reduces recovery times. For weeks following the first couple of surgeries, I was not allowed to get out of bed, much less attempt to walk, even on crutches.

As far as I was concerned, my life as a physical person — fond of cycling, baseball, hunting, and, best of all, fishing with Aurora Finn — had come to an abrupt close the second I crashed into the grass of my grandmother's backyard. I had little hope, and virtually no ambition other than developing all I believed I had left — thus embarking on a life of the mind that continues even now. Meanwhile, the rest of me — what should have been a strong, tall adolescent quickly becoming a young adult — became haggard and wraithlike. By the time I went away to college, I carried less than 130 pounds on a fragile 6-foot-3-inch frame.

But not all hope was lost. I saw this one day when I was 14, when Aurora came to visit me in the hospital. It was a weekend, and as usual when she was not in her parochial school uniform, she was dressed in her tomboy attire. That day, in addition to the chocolate malt she usually brought me from a restaurant across the street, I remember she left a book of Shelley's poetry on my bedside table. I thought it was a school book she had left by mistake until later that night, when I read what she had written inside. Though it was not a romantic note, it bespoke the bond we shared — both of us, in our own way, adrift and alone because of my injuries — expressed with 14-year-old profundity. "I need you to come home again, OK?" she wrote.

Aurora was very concerned about me.

"Well, this just isn't going to go," she had said that day, her slim frame curled up at the foot of my hospital bed as we talked about my prospects for walking again. "This just isn't going to go."

I didn't know what else to say and, as we often did when we were fishing, we passed a half-hour or so in silence, as she gently rubbed my right foot to see if I had any more feeling in it. If I hadn't been able to see her hands, I wouldn't have known she was touching me.

After we had watched part of an old "Andy Hardy" movie on television, Aurora had to leave. But before she got very far down the broad, noisy hall, she was back, standing at the door. "It's me again," she said. At first, I thought she was going to cry, which I had never seen her do. Instead, she climbed onto the bed again and inched toward me, past all the IV lines and the pillows that kept my squandered leg elevated, until we were nearly nose to nose.

"I'll get you out of here, Bobby Rose," she whispered, using the nickname I'd acquired a few summers before, when some stranger we'd met fishing misunderstood our languorous Southern accents when he'd asked our names. After awhile, even though my new identity no longer seemed so wildly hilarious, and once the maid at Aurora's house took to calling me that, it stuck.

I didn't know what to say, or how this would happen exactly. Somehow I just believed her, because Aurora always did what she said.

"You give me some time to think, Bobby Rose. You're gonna be well again if I have to teach you how to walk myself."

"What?"

"No, listen," she said. "We can do it because we're friends, OK? We're still friends, aren't we?"

"We're best friends," I said, the pain in my leg and my atrophied back throbbing as the last round of Demerol or Percodan or whatever it was started to fade.

"I thought so. I knew that was true." She put her arms around me, the first time she had ever done this, careful of the heavy back brace I lived in. It always seemed people were afraid to touch me after I was injured. I hardly knew what to do with a gesture like this, and she had let go by the time I'd raised my own arms to hug her back. Then she was gone, winking at me from the door like she always did.

Though it would take a very long time, and I would endure more operations and spend months in hospitals or bedridden at home, Aurora kept her word. With her help, and after the hospital therapists had done all they thought they could, I finally succeeded in standing for more than a few minutes at a time. And so it would be that a day or two before I turned 16, I took my first dozen steps, entirely on my own.

Aurora, who recently had undergone a sort of fashion transformation, had just come from school. She wore a long, pleated, navy blue dress and a wool coat and beret and gloves. For some reason, I remember her dark blue shoes with large silver buckles, which she always took special care to polish. When she helped me walk, our hands joined, I always watched her feet to gauge my own steps. Those shoes with the buckles made me think of someone old-fashioned like Emily Dickinson or Elizabeth Barrett Browning, whose poetry Aurora liked.

Often, I fell, sometimes quite badly, as my leg collapsed and my mousetrapped spine kept me from remaining upright. When she didn't manage to break my fall, Aurora, who was small but surprisingly strong, somehow helped me up again. Whenever we pieced our way along like this, I thought of the times when we ran or walked for miles through the fields and woods that were Aurora's true element. Now, with me reduced to a thin, trembling ghost, tilting along on my crutches, she walked as slowly as I did, her arms around me protectively, the only support I had.

The day I finally walked, we were in the park near my house. We were under some tall cypress trees, and there was the lightest breath of January snow in the air as the evening darkened and grew cold. As I limped along, my right foot dragging like an old sash weight in the frozen grass, she held out her arms to me. Neither of us had said a word, and I'd simply dropped my crutches and started toward her. By the time it was done, I felt I had staggered more than a hundred yards, but it had been only about 20 feet.

I can still feel her embrace gently closing around me when I finally reached her. For a long time, we silently held one another, the breeze around us icy and sharp.

"I'm going to teach you to waltz now, Bobby Rose," she said as I wept in her arms. "You can waltz me on my birthday in Memphis this year. OK?"

The first question people usually asked when they saw our family in the colony — for so seldom do people come and live the communal Hutterian way — is what were we doing in this place? What did we want there? How could we give up careers — mine as a daily newspaper editor in Fayetteville, Arkansas; my wife in the business office of a large regional hospital — to live without television or fashionable cars among a people who speak an archaic Austrian dialect and wear a blackcentric wardrobe that made us look oddly Old World?

This, even as we surrounded ourselves with the latest in farming technology and lived in houses that were well-built, furnished with handmade communal equity, and provided freely to all who lived here. To many, we seemed vaguely Amish, or, on the other hand, like members of one of those gun cults that spring up on the high plains once in a while and lie dormant until their darker motives shred their invisibility.

It's hard to give a clear-cut answer for any of this, or to convincingly explain our motives. To say we felt a true calling on our lives is only to hint at our motivations. But we very deeply felt a kind of biblical enjoinder to part with the ways of the world and follow our faith in community with others of a like mind and spirit. We reached a point in our lives as a family, both of us having come from backgrounds of privilege, where we felt it was required of us to leave behind the ambitions and goals we had always pursued and to look for something much more fundamental.

We were not the only people in the world to step aside like this, to look at life from an entirely different angle. We were just among the few to pick a place like this to do it, alone on the prairie among a people who had intentionally set themselves apart. By choosing this way, we were strangers among strangers, hidden in the riddle of our own anonymity.

It was a life that, aside from its benefits and blessings, placed us beneath a sign of great contradiction. In many ways, our life in the colony made no sense, and it never would, even to us. In one light, we were all impoverished, not even owning the shirts on our backs.

Our tax returns, because every man, woman, and child received an equal share of the corporate income, on paper at least, would seem ridiculous to anyone else. Our "income" of only a few thousand dollars each would not provide the most fundamental needs of survival, if that were what we really lived on.

However, we also were lavishly wealthy, beneficiaries of a large, prosperous, and well-managed corporation. We were millionaire farmers, a very small and selective gentry, much like the plantation owners who had been our milieu growing up in the South. In many ways, we lived like millionaires, too.

Nonetheless, because we lived communally, sharing corporate property in accord with the early Christians described in the New Testament book of Acts, we really could lay no claim to any of it. Everything – our houses, our land, our expensively advanced and fragile farm equipment, the hundreds of thousands of dollars we had in the bank – were regarded as transitory, even illusory. But illusions, as anyone who entertains them can attest, are often quite useful and enjoyable.

Other people who seek a different way, whether in religious orders or by intentionally dwelling alone, often nearly invisible to the rest of the world, have seen this contradiction in their own lives. Some escape it, while others embrace it by making it a special kind of burden. Somewhere along this spectrum lay the modest, mostly affable, and extremely well-set people we lived with. For six years, we were just like them, reaping the benefits of a treasure we were not even supposed to acknowledge could exist aside from the providence of God.

In our case, God provided extremely well.

We came to the community in December 1995, just a few days before Christmas. We moved there – my wife, Duann and I, both of us 31, and our two-year-old daughter, Shelby – from Fayetteville, in the Ozarks of northwest Arkansas, where we both had lived for nearly 15 years, most of that time as a married couple. I worked for 11 years at the daily newspaper there, starting out as assistant news editor and eventually becoming managing editor before I grew tired of the experience and our family made what could only be interpreted by most people as an act of total madness.

Duann and I, who had met in a theater class at the University of Arkansas, had been looking for something more substantial, even radical, in our lives for a very long time. During the early 1990s, with the birth of our first child, this wish for a greater purpose seemed to grow even more imperative. Because of an ongoing newspaper war and the regular exposure to the darker side of life that journalism sometimes offers, my work also was wearing thin and was deeply discouraging for me.

Fayetteville, which had been a very quiet, pleasant college town — except on Saturdays when the Arkansas Razorbacks played in the stadium there — had undergone quick, astronomical growth. This was due in part to the astonishing rise of the Wal-Mart corporation, headquartered about 20 miles away in Bentonville, and the election of our longtime governor, Bill Clinton, as president. Economic opportunity, and a housing boom that caused the city to spread far into what had formerly been scenic countryside, changed the landscape.

These changes also seemed to bring an uptick in violent crime in the area, which as a journalist I had some direct exposure to. For several years, Duann and I had lived in an old neighborhood near the UA campus, down the street from where Bill and Hillary Clinton had made their first home. We had enjoyed living there, but the night the police noisily raided a crack house just down our street, we knew it was time for us to move. At first, for another year or two, we lived at the very western edge of Fayetteville, in a house that overlooked a local car dealer's cattle pasture. Out our front door, we were firmly entrenched in suburbia, while out the back and down a slight bluff, we still had a glimpse of the woods and grassy hills I had come to love in the Ozarks. Occasionally some of the car dealer's cows would wander through the fence and into the street, and Duann, who grew up on a large cattle ranch in Kansas, would herd them back and I would staple the barbed-wire in place again.

The birth of our daughter also seemed to open in me a long-smoldering spiritual struggle. Though I had been raised Roman Catholic and attended Catholic schools, I had become little more than an agnostic – a former English and philosophy major who ascribed more to Wittgenstein and Spinoza than anything remotely biblical. I still believed in God, however, even if I had no way to articulate what that meant except in the most obtuse terms. At heart, as reflected in my education at the University of Arkansas, I was a poet and artist who had become a journalist to make a living, and for most of my life, Christianity had meant virtually nothing to me.

I had, and in many ways still have, what poet and novel-ist Jim Harrison has termed a "private religion." This reli-gion, which really isn't a religion at all, accounts for most of life's mysteries by holding them simply unaccountable, and yet assigns each person a measure of responsibility for all that occurs around them. It is an outlook that acknowledges and even embraces paradox, and yet is not alarmed by it. As a result, there is no immediate need for mediators, divine or otherwise, to usher us through any pearly gates or whatever we would face once that time came. Of course, the universe, being far greater than any of us, reserves the privilege to smack us down without warning, sometimes with the most comic irony.

For many years, this was how I looked upon life and its perplexities, having had most of my conceptions of hope and optimism fall into darkness through disuse.

For some reason, after Shelby was born, this changed. Dur-ing a rather serious bout with depression, in the aftermath of one of the blinding migraines I suffered several times a year, I asked my wife to drive me around one evening — I couldn't drive a car for nearly three years because of continuing spinal problems — until we could find a copy of the King James Bible. Something emphatic in me said I needed to find a copy right away. We quickly found out it was harder than one might expect to find a copy of the King James Bible on a summer evening in Fayetteville, but at last we did, quite late in a used bookstore in the UA's bar and recreation district.

In the weeks that followed, I devoured the Bible with great intensity. Though I still had nothing approaching real belief, I felt an inward change starting to occur. Because of my upbringing in the South, where fundamentalist Christianity was often the rural norm, I had always been very skeptical of spiritual awakenings. Stories I had heard of such experiences seemed crass and phony more than earnest. Along with one other man, a cropduster pilot, we were the only Catholics in our town of a thousand people, so I was used to being something of a spiritual outsider.

What finally turned my heart toward a deeper spirituality was a simple but quite cruel realization. For all my years of intellectual skepticism — which Duann, a devout Christian, did not share — I saw that my attitudes were beginning to affect others. Somehow, I knew that this would be a deeply grave offense, to ruin someone else's faith or belief, no matter what it was in, and I didn't want to do that to my wife or, for that matter, to our daughter when she got older. Even a "private religion" like mine regarded scandalizing someone else's faith as courting serious trouble.

Around this time, I remembered reading as a young man Thomas Merton's spiritual classic, *The Seven Storey Mountain*, which detailed his conversion to Catholicism and eventual entry into a Trappist monastery in rural Kentucky. Merton, who had been born in the French Pyrenees, the son of expatriate American artists, hinted at a life of great inner turmoil and even debauchery before, in his early 20s, he finally came to some degree of faith.

In many ways, not all of them literal, I shared Merton's experiences, and my spiritual evolution seemed very much like his. Soon, I went searching for a copy of *The Seven Storey Mountain* and read it again as well.

Like Merton, I had lived a rather amoral life before getting married at the age of 23. Marriage, and my job at the newspaper, had settled me down considerably. But not so long before, in college, I had been an avidly self-destructing lush, imbibing vast amounts of alcohol and remaining in some state of drunkenness — and once in a monthlong spell of total, overwhelming silence — for several years.

This illness had stemmed from a mental torpor that had been fueled in large part by the medical setbacks of my youth and by the staggering physical pain I still endured. This period of empty pursuits eventually cost me dearly in friends and companions in life. This included Aurora Finn, the closest friend I ever had, whom I had turned my back on in college despite her entreaties not to, an act of cruelty I would feel wretched and horrendous about for more than 20 years.

Because of the terrible pain and insecurity I had lived with for so long, I believed I was irrevocably broken, physically and emotionally. Bent on destroying myself, I felt I could never return the gentle care Aurora had always offered, born of the bond we had shared as children. The only thing I could bring myself to do was to isolate myself from her, and from most other people I had known, especially my parents and brothers.

Then, in February 2006, years after both of us had started our own families, Aurora and I met again, quite by chance, very far from both our homes, and she forgave me before I barely had time to ask her to.

She had seen me walking alone down a concourse of the Atlanta, Georgia, airport. She recognized me not from my much older face, but from the slight limp I still walked with, especially when I was tired, the limp she had seen for years as I struggled alongside her. Following as I looked for my gate, she watched me from a few feet away for several minutes before walking up from behind. Later, she told me she nearly gave up and turned away.

But her first words to me, whispered over my shoulder amid all the chaos of the airport, nearly tore my heart in two. It was how she nearly always said hello to me, a kind of password between us whenever we met. It had been so long since I had heard her quiet voice, I thought I was dreaming.

"Where you been, Bobby Rose?"

No matter what I had done to alienate so many people in my life, the link of our shared childhood could not be broken.

∼

My self-destructive bent continued unabated until I was in my last year of college, when I simply quit drinking, realizing that I had grown totally bored with that way of life, and with myself while pursuing it. This was not entirely easy, of course, and I had several setbacks before this self-imposed cure took hold. I was helped along in this by a strange and still unexplained physical change. Suddenly, my body became totally and violently revulsed by even the smallest swig of alcohol. This revulsion eventually relented, but by then I had quit my habitual drinking and gotten married.

I would only get seriously drunk once more in life — on an entire bottle of my faithful elixir, Old Bushmills Irish Whiskey — on Christmas Eve of 1989, a few years after I had started at the newspaper. That afternoon, the large holiday editions mostly put to bed, several of us had gone to visit a former city editor who was dying, slowly and painfully, of congestive heart failure in the Fayetteville hospital. Seeing this old colleague, who had suffered several strokes over the years, in such despair — literally gasping for every breath he took — knocked me squarely off the temperance wagon and into a liquor store on the way home. Duann was at her job when I got home and started in, but by the time she arrived later that night, I was in fully flung inebriation. The next day, nursing one of the few hangovers I'd ever had, I quit drinking for good.

Though it would be many years before I had any sort of spiritual awakening, much less moved to a Hutterite colony, I regard this experience as the start of my eventual faith, such as it is or ever was, and of the spiritual "journey" we would ultimately find ourselves on.

At some point in 1994, I realized I needed some sort of spiritual home. I did not want to return to the Catholic Church, for whatever reason, and I knew I did not want to go to any kind of mainstream church that seemed more like a social club. One church I visited, which was small and quite politically active, seemed interested only in my position at the newspaper — I edited the editorial page at the time — and the potential to use me to pursue their own social agenda. While I might have agreed with them on most matters, I knew I couldn't misuse the responsibility I had at the newspaper in such a way.

Amid all this, I remembered a brief trip I had taken to Montana as a teenager with some neighbors of ours — farmers who for part of the year lived up on the Plains. There, near the Canadian border, I had encountered their next-door neighbors, the members of the North Harlem Colony, the first Hutterites I would ever meet. Though this meeting was brief and rather inconsequential, they stayed in my mind for some reason.

Thus, when it seemed our family was looking for something new in our lives, I began corresponding with several Hutterite colonies, asking if we could come and visit and see what their lives were all about. At this point, I harbored few illusions about living in such a place forever. But one afternoon, a Saturday I recall, one of the colony ministers I had written to called our home. Duann answered, as Shelby cried quite loudly in the background. On the phone was the elderly minister of Starland Colony, David Decker Sr.

"It sounds like you're running a nursery there," he told Duann.

Later, when I got home from the newspaper, I called him back. We set up a time to come and visit, and later that month, in August 1994, I went to Starland for a week, followed in September by our entire family on another visit. We flew into Minneapolis and were met by the second minister, Herman Wollman, and several women from the colony who had come along to meet Duann and Shelby. As a gentle fall snowstorm began to blow in from the north, we made the 80-mile drive out to the colony, arriving just in time for Saturday evening supper. By the following Saturday, when we returned to Fayetteville, both of us believed we had found a place where we could live a very different, even radical, kind of existence. The day before, we had asked to come back and stay, and were told we could. Two months later, with our friends and some of our family deeply shocked and even angered by our unorthodox decision, we set out for Minnesota.

We arrived the next day just at sunset, the roads and ditches packed with several inches of snow and with more on the way that very night. The colony was decorated with a few strings of lights for the holidays ahead, and atop the 70-foot feedmill leg, a large blue-lit star shone for miles across the countryside.

Having followed our own kind of star — one that few other people could even imagine seeing — we arrived at the next part of our life, one that would last for almost exactly six years and which, at times, we thought and even hoped would never end.

That night it was 20-below on the blustery prairie, so cold even the stars and clouds and full moon seemed frozen. After unloading our belongings, the few we had brought from our former lives, we slept for the first night in the house that had been made ready for us. The next day would begin one of the greatest, and at times most frustrating and upsetting, experiences of our lives.

Before it was over, we had learned more about ourselves than about any of the people we lived with. We had also learned what it had been like to be alone, in many ways, among 100 other people — to be strangers among strangers. It was not always a bad kind of loneliness. But at times it seemed unabating, one of the hazards of living out on the prairie among a people who for the most part, even as an article of tradition if not actual faith, really wanted very little to do with people like us.

In this, Starland was different, because the people there accepted us, or at least allowed us to coexist with them for several years. On the other hand, looking back, I'm not sure I really knew anyone there, or that we allowed them to know us. We simply shared a portion of our lives together, and then moved on. More than a decade later, the experience seems neither good nor bad, just lonely, which doesn't have to be bad.

We probably weren't the only ones who felt that way.

chapter
FOUR

Nightwatch. 10:30 p.m.

Checking the metal shop, assuring that nothing has been left running inadvertently or too many lights left on. All overhead doors are closed and secured, although the main entryways are never locked, a point of contention among some of us in the community. If someone cared to, they could wait until the watchman was on the other side of the colony and quickly drive away with thousands of dollars in tools, computers, even food from the shop kitchen. Or, they could dash the unarmed watchman over the head and take their time.

Trailing melted snow behind me, I check a large industrial saw that has been set to cut narrow water pipe into precise lengths. Something in its inscrutable mechanism has gone awry, which is typical, so I leave it for the young man who will

arrive for work in the morning after breakfast. I punch the
large red "stop" button and the saw ceases its relentless hum
and goes to sleep.

~

I am totally alone amid millions of dollars' worth of high-tech metal working equipment, from a computerized laser cutter to press brakes that could bend an I-beam, or a hydraulic shear that could slice off an arm or a finger, or a head, in one swift blow. Alarmed by its resemblance to some mode of medieval torture — something the Hutterites were familiar with in their early history — I always give the shear a wide berth and flinch whenever its jolting blow falls hard and true, which happens a lot.

Everywhere in the shop, in any available corner and in an adjoining warehouse, are stacked immense pallets of stainless steel sheets, in all dimensions and thicknesses, the raw material we can never run out of. Because many of the steel merchants in Minneapolis happen to be observant Jews, the Hebrew holiday calendar plays a special role in the life of our community, or at least in the running of the shop.

Here, we know that when Yom Kippur or Hanukkah rolls around, or when the Sabbath sets in on Friday night, the steel merchants curtail their yards during the proscribed times. Accordingly, we plan so we never run out of steel, and haul tractor-trailer loads of extra supplies from Minneapolis whenever the ancient Mosaic calendar calls for it.

Most Hutterites know virtually nothing about Judaism. Once, I looked on as some Hutterites met some bearded, side-locked Hasids on an escalator in the Mall of America and mistook the Hasids for Amish people. History does not record what they thought we were. To some, we probably look like hayseed pioneers who must have stepped through a time portal from the prairie of the 1880s.

To others, we might resemble dusty convicts, wearing our dark coats and pants, which resemble a uniform of some kind. Hutterite women, on the other hand, with their polka-dot scarves and long, plaid-centric dresses, are often mistaken as being Amish or members of a convent. My wife, who normally is a rather vivid and outgoing person, said she was mistaken for a nun numerous times when she went out in her Hutterite clothes, which seemed to turn the most cheerful face into a mask of amiable concern.

Because of our steel business, some of us have, by necessity, become very well-versed in the cyclical aspects of Jewish life, which in a lot of ways resembles the Hutterian calendar with its holy days and religious festivals. This accumulation of obscure but useful knowledge is but one of the spices of life here.

In one corner of the shop, intentionally set a long way from my nemesis, the shear, stands the small and isolated enclave I call Welding World, where I spend several hours a week making small stainless steel parts with a thrumming heli-arc attached to an orange, man-sized tank of argon gas.

A perfectionist, like many welders, I am very particular about my tools. I make sure no one has "borrowed" my favorite canvas gloves — the fingers wrapped in silver duct tape until they finally fall apart — or swapped my delicately calibrated welding mask for another that no one likes. I also pass an eye over the myriad knobs and switches on the welder's blue control panel, making sure no one has come and jiggered around with my careful settings.

Then there is the row of needle-sharp tungsten electrodes I keep on my work table, next to the high-speed grinding wheel I use to hone them to a glimmering point. Whenever one goes dull, or turns up with a hardened blob of steel at the end — evidence a rank amateur has been on the scene — I can quickly reach for another and continue making the delicate, hairline welds I have become so mindlessly adept at reproducing thousands of times a day.

Someone figured out once that I make an average of 50 cents profit for each weld I do, so I am fulfilling my duty of making a lot of money for the collective. I have become known, among the company of occasional welders on the place, for the rather annoying habit of reusing my electrodes until they are only an inch or so long and scattered like pencil stubs on my table.

While they view this as a waste of time, I look upon it as a personal quirk, some part of the greater genius behind melting pieces of metal together. Somehow, I reason, my preening thrift with electrodes, which are not cheap, is directly linked to my success as a welder. It makes no sense, but I feel this way nonetheless.

My inquiry into welding began as a total innocent, never having approached a welder, or even a stainless steel part, much less a tank of argon gas, before coming to the community.

One day about two months after we had arrived in December 1995, the colony work distributor had a 15-year-old boy who mumbled whenever he spoke English instruct me in these obscure arts. With its vaporized metal "plasma" and potent electrical charge, welding seemed vaguely like the work of an

alchemist. The blinding sword of light that lashed out whenever the current hit the metal seemed primitive and vaguely
atomic, like the illumination that first filled the great void.

After a day or two, to everyone's astonishment, I was pretty
good at this new skill set. I was a natural, the work distributor proclaimed, preordained to wield the alchemist's crackling,
fatal wand. The job was mine.

~

*Everything tonight in Welding World looks normal and
unmolested, so I make my way to the stairs and offices on the
second floor, sweeping the walls with my official nightwatch
flashlight for good effect.*

*Picking my way up the creaky metal steps onto a precipitous
landing, I have one of those moments of immense doubt, a chill
of inner turmoil, or perhaps chagrin, that is usually as fleeting
as it is intense. I ask myself, as I sometimes do hundreds of
times a day: How on Earth did I get here?*

chapter
FIVE

The early 1500s were a time of great social and religious ferment. With growing dissatisfaction and rebellion against the long-established Roman Catholic Church, and what many perceived as gross miscarriages in its authority, the era known as the Reformation began to take shape. It would be a time of terrible suffering and martyrdom, as those who left the influence of the Catholic church-states in central Europe began to pursue their own interpretations of the Bible and the Christian faith.

Perhaps best known among the reform leaders was Martin Luther, an ex-Roman Catholic priest who started far-ranging protests and eventually established the Lutheran Church. Some, however, felt that Luther's efforts were not sweeping enough and began to form other groups that took even more steps away from the Catholic influence and dogma of that time.

In remote places, and at first in small numbers, people began to search and examine the Bible for its true message, which for so many years had been obscured by the Latinist forms of Catholicism.

In 1525, a group of three Bible scholars, Conrad Grebel, Felix Manz, and Georg Blaurock, met in Zurich, Switzerland, and soon perceived that true Christian belief was based on faith in Christ, made visible by an inner and outer conversion and regeneration of the soul from its sinful state.

The three discerned that infant baptism, as carried out by the state church, was invalid, and that only adult believers could be soundly tested in their faith and found deserving of true baptism of water and the Spirit.

After discerning this, the three confessed their faith and baptized one another. Very soon, others joined them, and this new movement led to the formation of the Swiss Brethren, and eventually to the Mennonites, who took their name from a former Dutch priest, Menno Simons. Their life was difficult and open to persecution and even torture and imprisonment from the Catholic leadership.

These believers were branded as "Anabaptists" by the Catholic and even some Lutheran authorities, because by accepting adult baptism, they had been "rebaptized" in the eyes of the state church, after having been christened as infants. The penalty, in many places, for being "rebaptized" was immediate arrest and eventual execution if people did not recant and go back to their original faith. Some were bent by the fear and pressure of arrest and torture and returned to the state church; others, however, were willing to pay the price to pursue their newfound faith. Hundreds and even thousands of these "Anabaptists" died in jail after long periods of deprivation and hunger. Others were beheaded or burned at the stake, not only for their belief in adult baptism, but because they refused to do military service or otherwise take up the sword.

Still, so great was their faith that accounts of their deaths reveal they went to their Creator with songs of praise and happiness on their lips, their hands raised in joyful prayer and exhortation. Others, with their dying words, forgave their tormentors, even as they held the flame to their feet.

From many of these early martyrs, we still have many moving letters of farewell and hymns written in prison to encourage one another and boost each other's spirits so that none would falter. Confined in their cells, the forebearers would sing loudly and join voices with their fellow prisoners, who could not be silenced in their belief, even by this violent oppression.

In 1528, amid all this turmoil, a handful of believers formed a group in Moravia (today, part of the Czech Republic) that went even further in its active life of faith. They formed a community in which everything was shared, following Christ's Biblical command to sell everything and follow him. They also sought to emulate the earliest Christian church in Jerusalem, which lived in total community of goods, sharing all property and claiming nothing as their own, as seen in Acts 2 and 4.

One account has it that the first group of believers laid all they had on the cloak of one of the men present. This, in the Europe of the Reformation, was the beginning of community of goods.

The new community grew and attracted many followers, led by the dynamic preaching of the ministers and what is recorded in accounts of the time as the simple, loving lifestyle of the brothers and sisters. The community members also endured much opposition. Still, the flow of new converts into the community, or "bruderhof," meaning "place of the brothers," was steady and came from all walks of life. One such person was an Austrian hatmaker, Jakob Hutter. Hutter was a man of zeal and deep faith who, according to church historians, held fast to the teachings of the Bible and was on fire for the way of community living.

Hutter pointed out some abuses taking place among the members, instances of property being held back for personal gain, of leaders feathering their own nests. After a serious struggle and reform effort, he was acclaimed as the group's new leader. Thus these people gained their Hutterite name, after the example of their early leader and reformer, a simple Austrian hatmaker. It is important to note, however, that Jakob Hutter is not regarded as the Hutterites' founder, nor did he lay the groundwork for the church. In the Hutterian view, that was done by God himself, who in the belief of the Hutterites is the author of a faith no human could ever establish.

Hutterite history books are filled with accounts of the troubles that followed the brothers and sisters wherever they went. During the time of Jakob Hutter's leadership, the communities faced all sorts of inner struggles, as well as horrible persecutions from the outside. All the while, more people joined the communities, relinquishing all they had.

Soon, persecutions became so fierce that many of the communities had to pull up stakes and flee, living at various times on the open heath and scratching the earth for the barest necessities of food and shelter. At other times, the communities were sacked and then burned, and the remaining people taken away to prison. In other places, the brothers and sisters dwelt in caves or even holes in the ground. Other communities were subjected to surprise attacks and the men, women, and children slaughtered in grievous ways. Still, the believers kept their faith and stayed together as best they could. Eventually, Jakob Hutter himself was captured and subjected to months of imprisonment, torture, and public mockery.

Finally, in February 1536, at Innsbruck, Austria, he was paraded through the Catholic cathedral, bludgeoned and bearing the marks of his tortures, some say with feathers stuffed into his brutal wounds. Then he was burned at the stake in the town square, an act commemorated with a plaque on the spot today. Over the years, Hutter was succeeded by other spiritual leaders who somehow kept the communities together, even in times of renewed persecution and flight. Among these were Peter Riedemann, Peter Walpot, Andreas Ehrenpreis, and many others, who all did their part to keep the Hutterian Church on the path of faith and community. Eventually, by the late 1700s, the communities had been chased again by persecution into the Russian Ukraine. Here is where they became more involved in agriculture than ever before, with the help of neighboring Mennonites who also enjoyed the freedom from military service extended by local authorities.

For many years, the early Hutterites lived in small villages in relative proximity to one another, but due to the long decades of flight and persecution and being uprooted, their dedication to community of goods had all but passed away, especially during the 18th and 19th centuries. One minister in Ukraine, however, Michael Waldner, a blacksmith, had a vivid spiritual vision in the 1850s — some say brought on by a blow to the head of the sort so ubiquitous to religious visionaries. This insight inspired him to reestablish community of goods. It was a slow and painful process, quickly compounded by other problems when officials in Ukraine no longer guaranteed the communities their previous military exemption. With migration to North America picking up from all parts of Europe in the early 1870s, Waldner and other church leaders decided to send a delegation to scout territory for the establishment of new communities in the United States. These scouts, sometimes in the company of immigrating Mennonites, traveled in the northeastern United States and the upper Midwest, finally focusing on areas in the Dakota Territory, Nebraska, and even as far south as Kansas.

After they returned to Ukraine and the migration was organized, the first groups set out for the United States. Eventually, after months of hardship and even numerous deaths on the arduous trip across the Atlantic, the first permanent community, called Bonhomme, was established near present-day Tabor, South Dakota, in 1874.

Shortly thereafter, other communities sprang up in the surrounding territory, along or near the James River, and in a few years, the Hutterian Church was established in the New World. This migration established the relatively small number of family names among the Hutterites, most of which are still found in the communities. These names include: Kleinsasser, Wurtz, Wollman, Waldner, Walter, Decker, Wipf, Maendel, Tschetter, Stahl, Glanzer, Ensz, Gross, and Hofer. Some names, such as Knels, have died out in the communities, while others, such as Baer, Benning, and Teichroeb, have come about because of converts.

Hutterian names also carry a couple of common courtesy titles, which usually imply a degree of respect for the person's age or position in the community. Among men, the word "Vetter" is frequently appended to a name. Though "Vetter" means "cousin" in proper German, in *Hutterisch* it means "uncle," though uncles are not the only ones addressed in such a way. To some people in the colony, I was known sometimes as "Rhodes Vetter" or "Robert Vetter." Our senior minister, David Decker, was known as "David Vetter" or, almost as often, as "Olevetter," which in *Hutterisch* means "grandfather."

Women's names feature the honorific "Basel," pronounced with an elongated "a" like the city in Switzerland. "Basel" means "aunt" in *Hutterisch* and is attached to names in the same manner as "Vetter," as in "Katrina Basel." I have never heard an explanation for the origin of this word, though it has been part of the Hutterite lexicon for more than 100 years at least.

My wife was often called "Du Basel," a shortening of her proper name, Duann, which also was frequently mispronounced, quite emphatically, as "Duane" because of the eccentric innovations of the *Hutterisch* accent. To many unaccustomed ears, this accent sounds less German than vaguely British, like the accents in certain parts of western North Carolina. Though "Vetter" relates to the *Hutterisch* word for "grandfather," the word for "grandmother" is "ankela," the origin of which also is rather vague. Some have linked it with the German word *engel*, for "angel," but this is not well established. Like many words in *Hutterisch*, it simply may have evolved over the centuries of migration and flight in Europe, growing out of loan words or local dialects until the original sources have become nearly obscured.

Bonhomme Colony, where these traditions and many others first took root in North America, still exists in far southeastern South Dakota, though the other original places have long since moved or been reestablished elsewhere. During World War 1,

Hutterites were no longer exempted from the draft, and a great struggle with the government ensued over the church's dedication to the peace witness.

Tragically, two Hutterite men died in the U.S. Disciplinary Barracks at Fort Leavenworth, Kansas, in November 1918, an event that only sped the progress of a large-scale migration of many communities to Alberta and Manitoba in Canada. Only a handful of communities, including Bonhomme, remained in the United States following this migration, and it was not until after World War II that any appreciable number of communities were reestablished south of the Canadian border. By this time, however, the Hutterian Church was broadly established in Canada, with communities focusing on agriculture and livestock and making a strong impression on both the national and provincial economies there. Indeed, their reputation as farmers had made them a welcome addition to Canadian officials.

A steady trend of growth ensued, made necessary by the simple expansion of Hutterian families and the need to branch out and form new communities from time to time. When Hutterian communities reach a certain capacity, usually around 150 people, leaders begin searching for a new place to start a daughter settlement. Gradually, as this new community is built up, families begin to move there and work the soil and continue the construction of houses, barns, and other needed structures. This is how nearly every Hutterite community was formed, as a daughter of another, more firmly established place.

The Hutterian life is set apart by its belief in and dedication to community of goods, the total sharing of earthly property, and reliance on others in the community to bear burdens and joys in unity and equality, at least in theory if not practice. The center of Hutterite life, however, is faith and devotion to God.

Though many secular groups have tried to establish communities, many have failed to achieve any longevity. In the Hutterite view, this is because they failed to include God in their way of life, as the center and focus of everything. Indeed, without God, the Hutterite thinking goes, it cannot be assured that people can live together and share the kind of life that the Hutterians share. Nor should any human try to take God's place in the Hutterite view, for this can only lead to disaster.

The Hutterites believe they have been fortunate to continue in this way of life for nearly 500 years now, despite setbacks, persecutions, tensions, strife, and spiritual struggles. Throughout it all, they believe God has chosen to preserve them.

Hutterite communities can be as diverse as they are numerous, but they also hold to some basic customs, practices, and viewpoints that unify them and lend them all a certain sameness. Communities are typically very open and friendly to outsiders, provided the visitors are there for a good reason and have not come out of idle curiosity. Most visitors are respectful of the Hutterian way of life and are invited to come again. Because many communities have reputations for being tight-lipped or standoffish, the level of interaction with non-Hutterites might be surprising to those who aren't members.

After they arrived in North America in the 1870s, the Hutterites gravitated into three very distinct groups. This came about initially because the migration from the Ukraine occurred in different segments, and because three communities were originally formed in South Dakota, where the Hutterites put down their American roots. Now, however, these groups, while sharing beliefs and the other social forms and customs of Hutterites, are different in many ways, particularly in the styles of their clothing. They also have a few customs peculiar to their own groups. The group known as the *Schmiedeleut* (or "Smith People") lives in Minnesota, South Dakota, North Dakota, and Manitoba in Canada. They are called the "Smith People" because their first leader in North America, a visionary minister named Michael Waldner, mentioned above, was a blacksmith.

The *Dariusleut*, named for their early leader Darius Walter, live in Montana and the state of Washington in the United States, and in Alberta, Saskatchewan, and British Columbia in Canada. In recent years, a Darius colony moved from Montana to North Dakota because of poor farming conditions.

The *Lehrerleut*, named for Jakob Wipf who was a schoolteacher (or *lehrer* in German), also live in Montana, and in Alberta and Saskatchewan. Though members of all three groups view themselves as Hutterites and embrace very similar if not identical cultures, the years have brought several small schisms within the three groups, as happens in most churches. And while efforts to unify the various groups have been made, most leaders have seen no need to make this step. Common among all Hutterites, of course, is the strong belief in and reliance on community of goods, as well as the peace witness. So while differences do arise from time to time, these tenets of Hutterite life seem never to vary or disappear.

Though it follows a somewhat rigorous schedule, daily life in a Hutterite community can also be quite spontaneous and full of surprises. At all communities, members are called to breakfast around 7 a.m. This is done either by a bell or some other signal. Community members soon assemble in the colony dining hall, where they sit in their assigned places and wait until one of the ministers, or another adult male, with hands folded, asks a quiet blessing on the meal before them.

(In some communities, the ministers eat at home, following an old tradition.)

Meals are usually eaten in relative quiet, to show reverence for the gathering and to maintain order, but this can vary from place to place. Indeed, while some communities might pass their meals in almost absolute silence, others might be much more active, with an atmosphere of talking and visiting, which, if necessary, is held in moderation by one of the ministers.

At Starland, meals tend to be more raucous than reverent, though in other colonies we visited, an almost monastic silence seemed to settle over the dining room.

Breakfast, or *frühstück*, lasts about a half-hour and ends with a prayer of thanksgiving. Then, everyone departs, leaving the kitchen crew to wash the dishes and clean up and begin preparations for the next meal.

A short time later, around 8 a.m., work in the various departments begins, and the children walk to the community's school for the start of classes. Adults enjoy a break around mid-morning for coffee and visiting, followed by more work until noon, when the entire community adjourns to the dining hall again.

Following dinner, there is usually a half-hour siesta, a *mid-dachstund*, with work resuming at about 1 p.m. At midafternoon comes another pause for coffee and a snack, followed by the resumption of work until about 6 p.m.

Shortly after the end of work, the community is called to the evening prayer service, or *Gebet*. This service, lasting about a half hour or 45 minutes, is simply a shorter version of the regular Sunday gathering and includes a hymn, usually in German, a brief sermon or reading, and a communal prayer led by the minister.

This time is seen by many as one of the most important and moving events of the entire day, with most of the community coming together after their labors and ending the day and its joys and problems, if not entirely in unity and peace, in the presence of God. Following *Gebet*, members again gather at the dining hall for supper, and then return home and spend the rest of the evening in various pursuits until bedtime. This period, depending on the season or the community's needs, may be spent in socializing or in additional work, such as when the harvest is on and the tomatoes need picking or when another work department has a big job to complete.

This schedule may vary somewhat from community to community, but is generally the one followed. In some communities, work on Saturday might conclude at midafternoon, and a period of hymn singing may follow supper. Saturday night also sees preparations for the Sunday morning service, along with family gatherings. Sunday, of course, is spent as a Sabbath and follows a much more restful, peaceful pace, centered around the day's worship. Many use the time of rest on Sunday afternoon to read the Bible or other spiritual works, including old Hutterite writings, or to otherwise reflect on the spiritual side of life in community.

Despite this apparently rigorous schedule, however, there is a good degree of spontaneity in the Hutterite day. In the afternoon, for example, a group of women might go shopping in a nearby town, or a work group might go for a short fishing trip. Some communities also assist in local nursing homes or in homeless shelters in nearby cities. Organizing play and work with children can also lead to some spontaneous changes in the usual schedule, changes that are almost always filled with the kind of joy and ease that the Hutterites believe only community living can afford in this day and age. Visiting at other communities, especially on weekends or holidays, is another popular pursuit and promotes unity and fellowship among various colonies and their congregations. These visits also allow the people, many of them relatives, to catch up on personal news and get to know new additions to the various families.

Typically, most Hutterite communities have a very similar appearance. Usually, long rows of residential houses form a quadrangle around a large common yard, which may be partly occupied by a long kitchen and dining-room complex. There is also a school on each place, which sometimes includes the simple, unadorned church meeting room. Otherwise, the communities look like most other large farms, with numerous barns, outbuildings, and storage facilities, as well as whatever shops or other work areas the community might require.

There is almost always something under construction in a Hutterite community, too, be it a new house or a remodeled hog barn. The communities are always located in the countryside, usually several miles from the nearest town. This is to emphasize their rural way of life and to remind the community members that the ways of the world are not for them. By living away from many "worldly" temptations, they hope to guard themselves against the occasion for many sins associated with "worldly" living.

Typically, most Hutterite communities are engaged in agriculture or agri-related trades and businesses. The majority of communities farm field crops or raise livestock or both, though others are starting to diversify into manufacturing and other pursuits.

Hutterite farms are usually large and employ the latest labor-saving equipment and implements. Just like other businesspeople, they do not shy away from high-tech know-how when it can benefit their communities and livelihoods. This is a key difference between the Hutterites and the Amish, who, though related to the Hutterites by way of the Reformation and a similar mode of dress, are dedicated to non-mechanized living and farming.

One reason so many communities are diversifying is because with all the added technology, fewer people are required to carry out traditional farming or livestock work. As a result, the colonies must turn to other areas of business, not only to support themselves, but to keep everyone meaningfully employed. This has led to some communities entering the metal-crafting industry and getting into smaller-scale enterprises. The main point, however, is that the communities must work to support one another and the needs of the community, which in the Hutterian outlook is a reflection of their love for one another and of the compassion God has shown them from their beginnings.

Most Hutterite communities have two ministers. These ministers are elected for life from among the baptized male brotherhood. They bear responsibility for the spiritual welfare of the community, as well as overseeing aspects of the colony's temporal needs and business interests. The head minister is usually an older, more experienced minister, while his assistant, or second minister, has been in the ministry a much shorter time. In many communities, the second minister also serves as the German School teacher, or sometimes as the gardener. The second minister often works closely with the community's children and young people, organizing some of their work and helping them, as they get older and mature, on the first steps of their spiritual journey as Hutterites.

Having two ministers has a practical side as well. When a community grows and decides to branch out and form a new colony, one of the ministers will be sent to the new place to oversee the flock there, while the other will remain at the founding community. The ministers are joined by a steward, or business manager, who is elected to manage all the community's business affairs and handle all the financial and material assets. The steward also oversees major purchasing and the community's stores of goods, such as clothing, food, or other needs.

The steward is also known as a "householder" or, in German, *haushalter*. In some communities, he is known as the "boss" or the *Wirt*. The ministers and steward are assisted by a work distributor, or *weinzedel* (*Hutterisch* for "vinedresser"), who makes sure all the community's work departments are properly staffed and managed. Usually, the work distributor also oversees the community's farming interests, planning each year's crops and the cultivation and harvest.

These managers are assisted by two adult males known as witness brothers, who help them make various decisions. The witness brothers also assist in the community's spiritual side by helping monitor the welfare of different members and in preparing candidates for baptism.

All of these members work together in managing the community and, in cooperation with the rest of the brothers, vote on major decisions affecting the colony and its members. Serious decisions are made by democratic majority often after the men have had periods of discussion and reflection. Other positions in the community include the heads of the various work departments, such as the carpenter, poultry man, hog man, feed mill manager, shop supervisor, and other similar jobs.

Among the women, there is a head cook, who oversees meal preparation every day, and a housemother, who makes sure each household has the basic necessities, such as clothing material, certain food items, cleaning goods, and other needs.

Though not always, the head cook is often the steward's wife, while the housemother is the wife of the senior minister. Like all women in the community, both have the privilege of retiring from regular work assignments when they reach age 45, though not all exercise this option, especially if they are in good health or have children old enough to look after themselves and their younger siblings. In many colonies, the housemother tends to be an older, grandmotherly figure, though a younger woman, such as the second minister's wife, might assist or take over this work as the older housemother ages.

In order for such an operation to work, however, there must be a very deep and abiding trust and spiritual commitment to the community from each member. This sense of surrender to the common good takes the form of obedience to those in authority, considering the needs of others before the needs of oneself, and the giving up of control and ownership of personal goods and possessions.

As Christians, the Hutterites believe this is only possible because they have God in their hearts and souls. Hutterites believe their ability to live in community, and to share everything and exist in peace with one another, comes only from God himself. Forces that divide them, or that pull at the framework of the communities, are seen as being not of God but of Satan.

Therefore, it is only by surrendering to the common good that they believe they can exist as they do. If each one went about doing things his own way, there would be no cooperation, no sharing, and, eventually, no community. When Hutterites say they live in community of goods, they mean they share everything the community takes in. They also are expected to ensure that no person goes without anything he or she needs. As a result, there are not supposed to be any independent or isolated "have-nots" in the community. Still, in communities where the communal system has broken down or drifted from traditional practice, some members pursue their own interests, earning money for themselves and keeping it back from the colony. This is common in some colonies, though among communities that have devoted themselves to strict communal living, it is harshly rejected.

To Hutterites, the things of this world are fleeting, and beyond their momentary use, they have no value. The Hutterian forefathers had a word for this kind of personal and spiritual surrender, *Gelassenheit,* which refers not only to surrendering the will of the individual but submitting oneself to the will of the community.

chapter SIX

Nightwatch, 1 a.m.

Back in the pickup, I drove down the side of the shop building to the mechanic's shop, which had a grease pit and hydraulic lift, just like a fully-outfitted garage in town. Like the main shop, this one was kept unlocked and was filled with thousands of dollars of tools just waiting to be taken by some interloper.

From here, I passed through a narrow door into the large truck wash, and then into the biggest part of the entire building – the car park, where not only the colony vehicles but the large farm implements, including two very large Case combines and several grain trucks, were parked. All the cars and minivans were home by this hour, except for one van that had taken a load of people to a colony in Manitoba, and another car that a young man attending college in Mankato often kept near his house overnight.

Sometimes, especially during frigid weather when all the vehicles had to be kept inside overnight, this garage was packed as tight as a jigsaw puzzle. It was quite large, though, and once was used to host the one and only funeral that occurred at Starland while we were there. John Wipf was an elderly, retired minister from a South Dakota colony and had endured years of terrible illness and pain. But instead of isolating him in a nursing home, he was cared for around the clock by two bachelor daughters, Dora and Christy, who seldom left his side, especially in his final illness.

When Johnny Vetter died, the spring after we had arrived, the traditions of a Hutterite funeral unfolded almost automatically around us. A grave was dug in the colony cemetery after the frozen ground was warmed by burning haybales on top of it for several hours. A colony coffin-maker from Long Lake Colony in South Dakota came and helped Tom Decker, Starland's carpenter, make a suitable coffin.

A wake with several hours of singing German hymns was held in the church room overnight, with the colony members, all in black, seated around the open coffin along with relatives from other colonies. Johnny Vetter also had a large number of relatives who had left their respective communities, and these people came as well. They presented an especially poignant sight, especially the women, who came to the funeral wearing their old Hutterite clothes but in full makeup and with hairstyles that clearly were not in keeping with colony practice.

The next day, the funeral was held in the car park, which had been cleared out and lined with folding chairs for the well-attended service. This gathering was about the same length as a Sunday *Lehr* and was followed immediately by the burial, with several men carrying the coffin the 50 yards or so to the leafy, well-kept plot set aside as a cemetery, where the neat grave waited to become the colony's first. Later, a simple concrete marker would be placed on the spot.

Not long after the funeral, Dora and Christy moved into the empty side of our house, and in essence, we became part of one another's families. People in the colony used to joke that I had three wives, because it soon became my responsibility to take Dora and Christy to doctor's appointments or on other errands, as all the men did for their own wives. As our family grew, Dora and Christy were like older aunts or erstwhile grandmothers to our children, and their brothers from their home colony in South Dakota, Herb and Henry, like jovial uncles.

~

Back in the pickup, I make a pass through the yard between the shop and the feed mill at the colony's extreme northeast corner. Driving beneath the large metal overhang where the semi-truck scales and grain pits are located, my headlights capture several very large rats scurrying out from the metal grate where we dump corn and soybeans during harvesttime. Though our large outdoor grain bins are supposed to be protected from vermin, the mill's overhead bins sometimes get infested, leading to scenes like this one. I make a mental note to tell the mill boss about this tomorrow, though he probably already knows.

Parking outside the mill, I make a quick walk-through, past the office with its glowing weather computer, into the mostly empty warehouse, and into the small glassed-in booth where the mixing of custom feeds is managed by way of a totally homemade control board. The grain is fed through the tall elevator leg from the outdoor bins into the overheads inside. From there, the control board feeds measured amounts of the needed grain, plus various liquid additives, into a mixing pit where a huge steel ribbon can process large amounts of feed in only a few minutes. From there, the mixed feed is bagged in another device or loaded onto one of our auger trucks or semis to be taken to our customers. At times, the mill has had a variety of customers, but with out-of-kilter grain and hog prices, not to mention fuel costs, our customers primarily have been other colonies.

Every surface in the mill is dusted with a fine powder of ground corn, and it clings to anything that touches it. Even if I am careful not to sit down any place or scrape against a wall or door, I still manage to come out of the mill with several white smears on my denim convict coat.

From the mill, I drive about 50 yards to a long metal building that houses several of our smaller maintenance shops and, until recently, the kitchen and dining room. Entering at one end, I pass through a large garage-like room that houses our huge electric generator, which we use whenever the local utility power goes out, as well as an extremely old fire truck that our property insurance requires we have on the premises. This truck, which must have been more than 40 years old, was not capable of any great speed and carried several hundred gallons of water in its tanker.

~

Conrad Decker, the colony electrician, takes care of the fire truck along with his other assorted duties, and occasionally takes the truck out for a spin, to make sure it still runs, or to use its high-pressure water hose as a kind of improvised Zamboni, such as ice arenas use, smoothing the colony skating rink during the long winter months. Conrad, a confirmed bachelor in his late 40s, was often surrounded by children in those days and would drive the truck around with a load of kids whenever he went on one of these shakedown cruises. The truck's rather raucous siren was the children's favorite feature and was deployed nearly constantly whenever the truck was on the road, and sometimes when it wasn't. I recall several times hearing people complain that our fire truck was virtually useless, and that it might be more effective simply to drive the truck into a fire and abandon it there than to use it to extinguish flames.

~

Through another door I enter Conrad's electrical supply room, and then his repair shop, which is crowded with any number of children's school projects, along with all manner of electric motors and machinery from around the place that need repairs. Conrad also made up a small cot in a room off to the side where he went for naps at odd hours. Because he is a bachelor and works mostly on his own, Conrad keeps his own timetable and can be found out and about as often at night as during the day.

~

If he was not in his electric shop, Conrad also could be found in one of the colony greenhouses, where he tended flowers and hydroponic garden plants year-round, including two pygmy banana trees he had kept going for several years. Whenever visitors came to the colony, especially outsiders, Conrad's banana trees were a favorite attraction, and when they bore fruit, it usually was sweet and tasty.

At various times, Conrad also kept a menagerie of animals in a large paddock at the south end of the colony. In addition to some Arabian horses, peacocks, rabbits, chickens, geese, and a few other temporary additions, there also were a couple of emus. Where these came from, or why, I never knew. But later, after they ventured into the horses' paddock, they were both killed by one of the horses, who kicked their heads off in full view of a group of children, including Shelby. The emus were gathered up by Conrad and taken to the kitchen basement, where he butchered them and cooked their rather flavorful meat on a small electric grill. That evening, the emus were fed to the *kleine-schul*, or "little school," children and whoever else wanted to try some. Not surprisingly, everyone agreed they tasted much like chicken.

Though Conrad was known for his way with animals, he also found them frustrating at times. He liked to tell a story about a colony rooster that would perch atop a rain barrel near his bedroom window and crow at inconvenient hours. One night, fed up with the insomniac bird, Conrad went on the attack, grabbing the rooster by the neck and forcing it under the water in the nearly full rain barrel. He might have actually drowned the bird if he had not looked down and seen the angry, belligerent look in the rooster's red, upturned eye. Seeing this, Conrad started to laugh uncontrollably and lost his grip on the chicken, which then escaped. Whether this actually happened, or happened in this precise manner, is hard to tell. I heard several versions of the story over the years, but the rooster always prevailed.

As a bachelor, Conrad, like our neighbors, Dora and Christy Wipf, and his youngest sister, Marion, were part of a significant circle of unmarried adults among the Hutterites. Nearly every colony we ever visited had at least one or two singles, some of them quite advanced in age. This was simply an accepted part of Hutterian life, as was the occasional late marriage for some, especially women, who had long passed the usual age for finding a spouse. Unfortunately, among Hutterites, a woman tended to be regarded as an "old maid" after about the age of 24, which represented a significant drop in her marital stock. Though some never gave up hope of marrying someday, Conrad clearly enjoyed his loner's independent existence, free of most household obligations.

~

From Conrad's shop, I pass into the former kitchen and dining room, which a year or so ago had moved into a new, larger building constructed for that purpose at the south end of the place. The large, open rooms were now used for storage and contained all sorts of odds and ends, from unused or discarded furniture to abandoned kitchen equipment, which had been replaced by brand new ranges and ovens in the new building.

Sweeping the room with the official flashlight, I see nothing amiss and head back to the pickup.

Even though the new kitchen is much nicer and far more convenient for the cooks to use, I felt a sentimental attachment to the old one for some reason. It had been the place where we had first come to share meals with the rest of the community. On one of her first visits to the colony, in early 1996, my mother had also played a classical piano recital there for the community one night. After performing several pieces ranging from Bach to Satie, she took a dozen or more hymn requests, and the gathering went on well past midnight.

~

Though colony life would not have agreed with her, my mother was a very popular visitor. On her first trip, she arrived amid one of the worst blizzards the area had seen in years. By the time we returned from the Minneapolis airport, the snow had drifted more than hip-deep in front of our house.

After we considered several ways of getting her into the house — including a plan that involved passing her through our living room window — we managed to get her around to the side door, which someone inside, probably one of our children, had to kick for several minutes to clear the accumulated snow. I recall that on that visit, my mother never ventured out again until several days later, when the snow had abated and started to either melt or blow away. Once she emerged, however, she quickly seemed to acclimate to the depths of the cold and early darknesses that made winter on the prairie so memorable.

While my mother made several visits to Starland — my father had died in 1986, so she was alone — Duann's family only came to see us a few times. Nevertheless, we maintained regular contact with them by phone and mail, especially as our family grew with the arrival of our daughter, Lydia, and son, Aidan. Duann's father, as a lifelong rancher, especially seemed to enjoy talking with the colony steward, David Jr., and we knew that when their weekly phone call came to us each Sunday, it probably had gone to Junior's house first.

chapter
SEVEN

Some time ago, I read about an Ethiopian monk who, as recently as the 1960s, had lived alone in a cave in the Egyptian desert, not far from an old Coptic monastery at Wadi al-Natrun. The various accounts attest that he lived in his cave, entirely isolated and shunning visitors, for several decades — a modern-day legacy to the austere and yet strangely luminous desert fathers of the early centuries of Christendom. Just when we believe such people no longer exist — either in the desert, or in the windy walkups of New York City — someone comes along to prove otherwise, showing quietly that unbeknownst to most of us, men and women are still doing the secret work of heaven.

This solitary Ethiopian endured more than just the deprivations of the desert along his unmoving journey. In World War II, he was fired upon by the advancing German panzers of Erwin Rommel, and then, with the Allied invasion a few years later, by the British and American cavalries, who later learned what they had done and, with grand English manners, apologized for interrupting his solitary retreat.

As if he cared. The hermit later told a rare interviewer he had thought the tanks and howitzers were only the distracting minions of Satan. He had brushed them aside as merely the vague illusions of hell and nothing more. He knew, it seemed, nothing of the war around him, even when it madly processed in front of his eyes. Or, he may have known everything of the war and seen it in its precise and true nature, without shadows.

But what was this man doing all that time? What was his mission? Some would say it was worthless, meaningless, perhaps even blasphemous, because there are always people who say things like that. But perhaps this man's life was a model of surrender and a testament to the vitality and grace of the human soul. Perhaps, in days like these, we need such people more than ever.

Each night, without fail, the monk would emerge from his cave and, facing east, raise his hands and begin a long litany of prayers for the world and everyone in it. When he was not standing, he was kneeling or prostrating, or lying face-down in the sand, his prayers unceasing. But most of the time he stood there, hands uplifted, gazing skyward into the splendid and eternal universe, and doubtless helping to hold the world together with his petitions and supplications. When the sun eventually began to break above the horizon ahead, his night-long vigil would end, and the hermit would go back into his shelter until the following twilight called him forth again.

Ever since I read this account, I have wondered what this solitary man prayed for, how he reached from deep within his soul to ask redemption for others, how he shed tears for the vast and unknowable suffering that happens in this world every minute of every day.

One night in winter a couple of years ago when I had the watch, I tried just that, standing in the snow in a dormant cornfield at the edge of the community. I stood far from the welcoming lights of our place, freezing in the desperate air of the new winter, with a chiding frisson of apprehension and unworthiness as Orion and the Pleiades twinkled overhead.

Mostly I was just cold, so no real holiness surrounded me that night. I wouldn't even call what I did praying. But for a moment or two, when the wind would grow still, I felt a part of something far greater and encompassing than those snowy fields, or the distant lights of Minneapolis. Another place, not known to many, seemed very close at hand, as if angels stood in the eaves of our houses, atop the grain bins, along the beam of the long dark barns, arrayed like frigates on the prairie.

The community is a privileged place to dwell in, especially when we approach God in this way. What we pray for usually defies the prisms and mirrors of words, yet still finds its way forward from our heart.

What then do we ask of the God of silent turning galaxies, the God of shivering dark and forests and cornfields, the God of cold and ice?

What do we ask of the God of unbreakable promises, when we are confronted by our own evil and by the evil of those around us? There is little to ask, except what the publican asked and what the Ethiopian hermit must have certainly asked beneath the numberless stars and sky of the Egyptian desert. They are eternal petitions, immutably fused with suffering souls everywhere: *Here we are. Forgive us. Have mercy on us. Save us.*

We all know these petitions, especially we who have lived a common life with other people, who have been part of a visible community of saints — such as saints are here on Earth.

I was often reminded, living in the colony, that a large part of my own spiritual journey has been a consideration of how to be alone with God. I think of this in some ways as akin to the solitude of the desert hermits, past and present, or of the Hutterites alone together on the prairie, or of the wandering dervishes of Morocco or Bosnia. I think, too, of the mountain solitaries of China and Japan: Cold Mountain, Basho, Ryokan, whose poetry still dashes my spine with wind and stars and ice, ever since I encountered them more than 20 years ago.

Not that I possess any abiding holiness to speak of, certainly none that could compare to these. But such are the ones I look to — for inspiration, for courage — a colloquy of hermits and poets and solitary travelers.

chapter

EIGHT

Hutterite communities are known for the long, multiplex buildings that house their members, who still often have rather large families, despite a general trend toward fewer children. Indeed, Hutterite families are the focus of the colony's daily life. Hutterite children, after all, are the future of the Hutterian way of life, and like many parents, Hutterites want to cultivate in them the proper respect and devotion to the ways of God and, ideally, community living.

Marriages in the colonies take place amid much celebration. Usually, a young man chooses a wife from another community. This is because most people on one place are quite often related. Their time of getting to know one another is not like in the world, however. Here, choosing a marriage partner is carried out, to the Hutterite way of thinking, in the fear of God and with the church's counsel. This does not mean that some young couples do not fall prey to the same urges and temptations as couples outside the colony.

But with the church's close observation, the chances of this are greatly reduced and marriages are, it is hoped, built on a foundation of fidelity and Christian faith. Once a couple becomes engaged, their marriage usually follows shortly after, at the groom's community, where the couple typically live following the nuptials.

As strict matters of faith, Hutterites only marry other Hutterites, and they do so for life. They must be baptized in order to marry and established as full members of the community. Contrary to some myths, the Hutterites do not arrange marriages or otherwise broker couples into marrying one another. They also do not permit remarriage after divorce, unless the other spouse has since died, so special care is taken that each one chooses what a Hutterite would consider his or her proper, God-given spouse, and that they live in an atmosphere of faithful devotion to one another. Once a couple is married, or soon after, they will be provided with a home of their own, along with all the furniture and other goods they will need to establish a household.

Often the bride will bring a number of favorite items from her home community, in addition to her various personal effects. The couple also receive numerous gifts from friends and relatives, to assist them in making their new home. Hutterite houses usually consist of several bedrooms and a living room, and sometimes a small kitchenette (a full-scale kitchen is not needed because most meals are taken communally).

The furnishings are usually kept as simple as possible, though colony homes are not totally without decoration. Most communities have individual, private dwellings for each family, though a small number have large, apartment-style buildings with shared entryways and common areas used by more than one family. This style is patterned after the earliest Hutterites in Europe, who lived in similar homes. Communities with these kinds of homes feel the communal lifestyle is more fully emphasized in this way. Most places retain individual homes within multi-family dwellings, however.

While Hutterite children are the future of the Hutterian faith, a colony's old people are the church's wise and priceless treasure. Hutterites love and value their elderly people throughout their golden years, and they go to great lengths to care for them and give their lives the dignity they deserve, even amid great or persistent illness.

Elderly people are given work to do if they feel up to it, and they are always provided with proper medical care. They remain a vital, important part of every family as long as they live, and they are looked to for advice, support, and guidance. It would be unthinkable for a Hutterite community anywhere to treat its elderly people with the disrespect so often seen in the world, or to neglect or shun any of its members just because they are of advanced age.

Hutterites believe that this would be to break several of God's commandments all at once, not the least of which is the commandment of love for one another. The same love also is extended to those who are sick, at any age.

All Hutterites speak English, of course, and are schooled in High German to help them understand and take part in their traditional worship, which includes many old German hymns and sermons. But they also brought with them from Europe a varied, quite complicated dialect that they speak in day-today life in the colony and which their children often learn as a first language.

The *Hutterisch* dialect is a combination of Tyrolean (for the area in Austria where many Hutterite families originated), Carinthian, and High German, with elements of Russian, and now English, mixed in. The *Hutterisch* dialect is a veritable road map of all the places the Hutterites have lived over the centuries, from Austria to Transylvania to Ukraine and North America.

Most people who can speak German can understand at least part of the *Hutterisch* dialect, but some expressions remain quite inscrutable. As it is not a written language, there is no standard syntax, vocabulary, or spelling, and therefore, no accurate or at least consistent pronunciation. To the outsider, this complicates the process of trying to understand, much less learn, *Hutterisch*, though a few converts to the Hutterian faith have managed to pick it up eventually. Interestingly enough, modern-day Hutterites who have traveled in Europe, especially in Carinthia and Tyrol, find a form of the *Hutterisch* dialect still very much in use and easy to communicate in. Apparently, the dialect has not changed that dramatically since the Hutterites left those regions hundreds of years ago, other than acquiring new words or expressions from cultures beyond their Austrian-Moravian homeland.

Hutterian clothing is perhaps what sets the colony dwellers apart the most as a "peculiar people" of God. Though Hutterites do not dress identically, they do follow certain rules regarding their attire, which they value for its modesty and homemade simplicity.

The men and boys wear black trousers, shirts with buttons or snaps, and suspenders. Feed caps or similar hats are worn by most of the men, while the ministers wear modest black hats, either fashioned from straw or beaver felt, similar in style to the hats worn by some Old Order Amish. In far Western colonies, such as in Montana or the prairie provinces of Canada, black cowboy hats are often standard for the men and boys. Other clothes, such as jackets or coats, are usually of a dark color, with no bright patterns or flashy decorations.

At or after marriage the men grow beards, which they wear the rest of their lives. The Hutterites believe that because God made men with beards, they should not shave them off once they reach maturity. They are kept neatly trimmed, however, and not worn long and bushy like many Amish men do.

The women and girls wear long dresses of a modest cut and pattern, and, after a certain age, the traditional black, polka-dotted head covering. (The women cover their unshorn hair in obedience to biblical teachings.) Girls' dresses are sometimes more colorful, as are their bonnet-like caps, but all women's clothing is modest, conservative, and generally of a similar or identical style. Neither men nor women wear jewelry, though in some communities, plain gold wedding bands are allowed for the women.

The purpose of this attire is to show modesty as Christians, and to show that by adopting a unified dress, the Hutterites are all together as believers and as members of their communities. Beyond this, these clothes are not regarded as "holy" or of any religious significance. They carry no special power or grace, any more than any other piece of cloth can be endowed with otherworldly powers. Hutterites dress as they do to go modestly before God, and, they believe, to offer no moral distraction to others by their appearance.

Hutterite communities each have their own colony school, either supported as a satellite public school or as a private parochial school. Most Hutterite children are educated from kindergarten to 8th grade, though with growing technology and a more diversified life in the communities, some colonies are finding high school, and in some cases college training, to be of great benefit. Starland was in this group and had several college graduates when we lived there.

Hutterite children begin their education in the communal *kleine-schul*, or pre-kindergarten, which takes children at age 2½ and starts with teaching songs and other activities. The children play, eat, and nap together, and in this way begin learning about communal life, from the basics of sharing to praying at meals to working together and cooperating.

After *kleine-schul* comes kindergarten, which actually is a Hutterite innovation dating to the Hutterites' early days in Europe. In that often turbulent era, some of the first kindergartens were founded in Hutterite communities, and quite often, rich noblemen would send their children there, and to the regular Hutterite schools as well, so positive was the Hutterites' reputation.

In that time, Hutterites were often very highly educated people, with a number of doctors and skilled artisans among the ranks of every community. Today, Hutterites are starting to see that their avoidance of what they consider worldly wisdom in modern-day schools may have to be tempered with some of their ancestors' appreciation of higher education.

Today, Hutterites are finding that if it benefits the community, they should send some students on to college, if what they will learn will be of genuine use back home. Usually, those who do go to college travel only a short distance and return home each night, or live at a Hutterite community near the college during the school term. This way, the colonies do not have to send their young people to live in unfamiliar surroundings where Hutterian values would not be observed.

Following kindergarten come the regular elementary grades, which are taught much as in any other school. This "English" school is usually taught by one or more outside teachers, though more communities are training certified instructors of their own. They also incorporate in their daily curriculum the traditional German School, where the German language is taught alongside Hutterite religious beliefs, history, songs, and other faith-related subjects. In this way, the Hutterites find they can keep alive their history and instill in their young people an interest, and even a longing, to know about the lives of their ancestors.

NINE

To be alone with God, one does not have to be entirely isolated. There often can be others on the journey as well. In my own case, I had a wife of nearly 20 years and three small children. Taken together, we were a bit of a crowd. But standing apart as we did from the world, we were quite distinctly alone, even as we followed a path shown to us only one step at a time. For many who find themselves alone, life can be a great social and spiritual burden. But for us, we found considerable purpose in being part of something different.

Once, a visitor to our community said that it was important that we all were there, doing what we did, even if we – knowing our many faults – disagreed with that. But in cases like this, grace may be in the beholder's eye after all. God still used us, no matter our sinfulness and wealth, which we denied even as we seemed to thrive on its many benefits.

After all, it was *our* wealth, held as a selfless, if autonomous, collective, and not *mine*, as in the reviled and altogether disreputable world. It was a kind of ghetto mentality at its most pronounced, and on this night, my task was to keep watch over our delightful encampment and to protect it all from all harm while it slept.

"There should be more people like you," visitors to our community often told us.

Well, no, some of us wanted to say, especially me. There really shouldn't be.

~

Several months after we had moved to Starland, a period during which we had passed a long and dormant winter, seldom traveling because of the deep and smothering snow, I made a trip into the Twin Cities, about 80 miles away.

Having lived so far from the rest of society, even for a few months, I felt a distinct anxiety when I found myself in downtown Minneapolis that first time, navigating the crowds and passing among buildings much taller than our colony's feed mill leg, which was the tallest object in all of Sibley County, taller even than the competing twin spires of the Catholic and Lutheran churches in the next town. Maybe that was our steeple.

Those few hours in Minneapolis reminded me of what the rest of the world was really like — a place of astonishing wonders, but also of great suffering, the like of which we had no concept back on our dirt-road commune.

An encounter with the homeless, or the sight of a man and woman begging for money beneath an overpass while their small fire smoldered and snow drifted around them, filled me with despair and dread.

Returning to our place that night, down the snow-streaked county roads, past gray dairies and mailboxes with Norwegian names, I sat in David Vetter's living room. I told him I was glad I had such a place to come home to, that we didn't have to live like the people in the big evil cities, that we did not have to face the realities, grim or otherwise, of life, essentially, in the real world.

David Vetter looked at me a moment and said something I did not expect: "Spoken like a true Pharisee," he said. "You've only been here a few short months, and already you're getting to be just like us."

When we first moved to the community, I had told the people, "I have been looking for you for a very long time." In all modesty, I wanted to be exactly like these rather dark and taciturn people, gliding gently through their lives, barely disturbing the world around them — not to be told that I was already too much like them.

"Spoken like a true Pharisee," David Vetter told me. "Don't be like us, Robert. Actually, we were hoping we could be a little more like you."

This really took me aback. After all, we had come to the colony hoping to become more like the people we perceived as humble, giving Christians who left behind the world to share everything in peaceful equality. Now I was hearing that our minister wished his flock could be a more spiritually open and seeking people, and not tied so slavishly to tradition and habit for their sense of righteousness.

What a dilemma. We are all capable of being Pharisees, of course, and some of us tend to err on the pharisaical side more often than not. It comes to us naturally, like a kind of spiritual racism, something that has to be uprooted and burned away, replaced with a patient, compassionate wisdom that does not weigh lightly on most souls.

In the community we got lots of practice at recognizing this, and at failing to reform ourselves, usually when it mattered most.

Like this: One thing Starland never lacked was visitors. Each year we probably got two dozen tour groups who came to see what we were doing — which wasn't a whole lot sometimes.

We hosted schoolchildren, sewing circles, college classes, Lutheran aid societies, residents of a local nursing home, even some Seventh-Day Adventists who tried to convert us but soon discovered they had barked up an empty tree.

Some genuinely desired to know us. Others were only curious and came armed with strange, phone-prank-worthy questions.

They'd ask: For what purpose do the men wear suspenders?

We carry a lot of keys, I told one person.

Then there were the bizarre questions: "Do brothers marry sisters here?" or "We heard you eat your old people."

Despite this last concern, our visitors usually had dinner with us in our communal kitchen and then took a walking tour of our barns and shops and perhaps one of the houses. They were a hardy lot, these Hutterite-watchers. Nothing seemed to discourage them. They would walk as far as we asked them, and they endured with stoic stamina lectures about our "faith" and "lifestyle."

Then they would skitter across the ice in their high heels or penny loafers —snow seemed a constant in Minnesota, and everyone but us seemed improperly dressed — moving from barn to shed until at last they started looking at their watches and toward the road and thinking of what else must be done that day. The time of the world regained its gravity, and soon we realized our little moment of congeniality had ended. They boarded their buses or climbed into their sensible cars and were gone.

We were not the world's best tour guides or very exuberant missionaries. Some of us were con artists, selling loaves of homemade bread or sacks of tomatoes out the back door, so to speak. But some of us tried to do right, and these "world people," as we called them, seemed quietly satisfied, which left us with a dangerous sense of ever so slight superiority. But there was something even more troubling to be reckoned with.

Invariably, when our visitors were gathering themselves and their purses to leave, one of them would come up and say almost these exact words, striking at a deep and tender root of my conscience. I could see the words forming even before they were said, and I wished I could stop them before they reached our ears: "There should be more people like you."

The first time I heard this, I didn't know what to say. It was meant as a compliment, but what does it mean, really? "There should be more people like you."

More people like who? It made us all uneasy.

But why? Were we not true in our belief? Were we not striving to live a life of difference — or was that indifference — of simplicity, of genuine faith?

I felt this way mostly because we were humans and not role models for anyone, unless they were willing to live among one another's faults and differences and hang-ups and to do so in community — in very close personal and spiritual quarters. Spoken like a true Pharisee, once again.

But this was not what I meant either, for in this we were not unlike a lot of people who tried to share an earnest life, even a common life. I meant that instead, we should all strive to imitate Christ — who had no barns or shops or International Harvester combines and whose community was one of the road.

Instead of people like us, who were lazy and took too much for ourselves, and always asked how our interests would best be served, there should be more people like the radical, troublemaking Christ — the one who turned tables, purged temples, and brought forgiveness and hope to the sorrowful. When have we last done this ourselves? And let's not be too quick to answer.

Christ felt no sense of entitlement to society's riches. According to the belief of any Christian, he took nothing for himself but the sins of the world across all time and space.

Because of our Anabaptist values, people looked to us for something unique, even if they didn't know exactly what it was. In the colony, people looked at our communities, at our plain clothing, and believed they saw something true and meaningful there. But what was our plainness? Was it a virtue, a spiritual compass, a reflection of modesty and humility as it was meant to be, or merely an attribute? We should wonder.

But when we were praised by people for what we seemed to be, perhaps we should have been quick to admit what we were not. Or rather, admitted what we really were, like the remorseful tax man, Zacchaeus, in the New Testament, who was a sinner, perhaps more than a little dishonest, a small-time operator with a ruthless agenda. This way, people could see what Christians believe that Jesus has really done for them —

changing them from what they were, to what they are when they are truly themselves — a grace none of us can take credit for. Jesus said: If you're content to be simply yourself, you will become more than yourself.

This is one thing I learned in the colony. People most certainly were looking for us — for that which made us different. Even if we were not aware of it, the whole world was watching — the saints and sinners, whores and gamblers, fools, kings, immigrants, drifters, criminals, the scattered strangers flung to the curb, even us occasional Pharisees.

We had to remember that the difference other people sought was not us, or anything we did. It was the idealism of Christ and the mercy Christians believe he bestows. We're all going to need it, after all.

chapter
TEN

Though Charles de Foucauld is considered one of the most influential religious thinkers of the last century, every effort he undertook in his difficult, lonely life was essentially a failure, including his attempts to establish a Christian brotherhood amid the Muslim nomads of the Sahara Desert. It is nothing short of miraculous that God could take this life of disappointment — wrenched from wealthy dissipation and the darkest sins by a staggering conversion — and turn it to something of such great and incomparable inspiration.

Central to Foucauld's spiritual life was his core conviction: to live the impoverished "hidden life" of Christ in Nazareth, laboring, praying, and quietly exemplifying the Christian ideal, even amid a harsh, desperate, destructive landscape of war and wandering.

Sadly, no one ever came forward to share Foucauld's desire for community, and so his life was spent almost exclusively as a hermit, a rejected community of one, exploring the ancient ideals of the early Christians and delving deeper into prayerful seclusion in an increasingly hostile land.

Foucauld's dream of brotherhood was cut brutally short on December 1, 1916. With vicious hostilities flaring between Algeria's Muslims and the French outlanders, Foucauld found himself in a broadening shadow of danger. Hidden away in his fortified hermitage, which had room for many but housed only him, Foucauld was attacked one night by a band of Tuareg rebels. As the hermit quietly sat and prayed, a young, frightened Tuareg rifleman shot him through the temple, ending a journey that had started amid splendor and money and yet ended in loneliness, poverty, and the cruel surroundings of war. It was a death Foucauld foresaw and even seemed to expect as inevitable. More than once, he challenged his friends and correspondents, as well as himself, to live as if they would all be martyrs someday, probably sooner than later.

In our spiritual journeys, we don't consider martyrdom very much anymore, but this is also a part of the life alone, of being apart from the elusive safety of conformity. In the Hutterite world, martyrdom is still a possibility that seems real, especially to some of the older people. As recently as 1918, Hutterites were being tortured and killed for their convictions. In this case, it was two men who died in the dungeon-like U.S. Disciplinary Barracks at Fort Leavenworth, Kansas, for refusing to serve in the military during World War I.

This story is still a vital and immediate part of Hutterian lore; even many of the younger people know what you are talking about when you simply mention the men's names — David and Michael Hofer. On their graves in a windy South Dakota field, the word "martyr" appears beneath their names – something that seems antique and nearly inconceivable to us here, in this age, in this place.

In 1996, the Trappist monks who were kidnapped and beheaded by Muslim extremists in Algeria took the attention of the world for a little while. When this happened, one of the older members of our community in Minnesota, one who had been jailed as a conscientious objector in World War II, commented – quite seriously – that we could be next. Were we ready?

This was our shoe man and soap-maker speaking – an old turkey farmer and *besenbinder*, or broom maker, a lifelong Hutterite – and not a prophet. But he knew what he was asking and how it sounded.

Of course, that would be almost unthinkable, but how do we know? Certainly, those Trappists at Tibhirine, or Charles de Foucauld, knew there was a chance they could be martyred. They might have even had a very clear idea of whose hands would end their lives, and even when the final blow would come.

But the Algerian Trappists, like Foucauld, like any number of others who have been martyred, like the Hutterites whose people were killed in an American prison in World War I, chose to remain where they were. They stayed, maintaining their community and their ties to the people and the land around them, even though it would cost some of them their lives, and much else.

Is this our calling, too?

The central question we must ask, when considering our lives as believers, is what did Christ show us when he was here?

What kind of life did he model for those who would come after him? This question is at the heart of a movement like the Hutterites, or of the Mennonites, Amish, Brethren, or Quakers, whose peace witness still sets them apart from a large part of society.

Again, Foucauld felt he had a clear call to follow the true Christlike way. At the core of his theology - or more properly, his outlook - was an undying, uncompromising dedication to the living example of Christ on earth. Not content with a fair imitation of a Christlike attitude, or with a priestly approximation of desert piety, Foucauld wanted to live out in every way conceivable the literal and exact life that Christ must have lived as a man in Nazareth.

It was a life of poverty, deprivation, rugged survival, hard manual work, and, one might imagine, a certain kind of desperation to live one day after the next, seldom knowing where one's next meal was coming from - a desperation that Foucauld saw lived out around him by the impoverished desert nomads, and which he took upon himself as a sign of his devotion to Christ.

As a result, Foucauld was skeptical, even distrusting, of any other way of life, though he tried to accept and respect the ideals of those who could not, and wouldn't even think of trying, to accept or understand his.

"I am in the house of Nazareth with Mary and Joseph," Foucauld wrote. "Like a younger brother sitting opposite my elder brother Jesus."

This sense of being the "little brother," sincere and yet humbly in need of guidance and help, was also central to Foucauld's spiritual life. In the landscape of his harsh existence,

Foucauld too was a nomad, a spiritual sibling walking beside his guiding, saving, older brother.

From his hermitage in Algeria, he wrote, "My God, I do not know how it is possible for some souls to see you in poverty and themselves remain voluntarily rich, to imagine themselves so much grander than their Master, their Beloved, and not want to be like him in all things. I do not doubt their love for you, my God, but I think there is something lacking in their love. – I just could not do it, O God. I could not love like that."

Foucauld personified the "community of one," the one who seeks but is never joined on his difficult and crucifying journey. Our experience with the Hutterites was similar in some ways. Though we found ourselves with others who lived according to a code of communal altruism, few if any could relate to our own desire to live apart, to be a part of a radical community of resistance, of a place that made a difference, or seemed to. To most Hutterites, life in the colony simply was something they were born to, not a choice they up-ended their lives or abandoned ambitions to pursue. Still, like Foucauld, many in our community were unsettled by the fact that we were actually quite wealthy, believing it was bordering on dishonesty to be stewards of great wealth and yet claim to possess nothing of our own. As prosperous farmers, we also operated other enterprises that brought in a great deal of money. Though we owned nothing as individuals, per se, we were millionaires, every one of us, and most of us lived like it. In our community, no one lacked anything, and luxuries abounded, from well-appointed houses and farm equipment to the occasional European trip, ostensibly for business.

Sometimes, this wealth led to the usual kind of arguments that money can spawn. Whenever the community had to make a major purchase, the steward and ministers would talk it over, and then the male members of the colony would consider the expenditure and vote on it. Sometimes these discussions were astonishing.

On several occasions — say, when we were spending hundreds of thousands of dollars on some new farm implements, to build a new house, or to purchase additional land — the discussions could be quite brief and the vote almost taken as an afterthought. The meeting would seem to end only moments after it had begun, and I would walk out stunned by the carefree speed with which we had just spent such a large sum of money. On the other hand, relatively simple projects, such as deciding where to build a new pole barn or a metal storage shed, could unleash heated arguments that might drag into the night and even have to be continued in subsequent meetings before they were settled. Often, it seemed interpersonal conflicts or family jealousies would come to the surface in these debates.

Obviously, contention like this had deeper roots than mere financial considerations. But the nonchalance, the utter insouciance with which we would commit ourselves to such huge expenditures while niggling and even fighting over relatively minor undertakings, said something about us. These occasions showed very clearly how some of us regarded the resources we had accumulated and seemed to expend at times so casually.

ELEVEN

Most people in the world cannot imagine giving up all that they have and surrendering their life and even their general sense of free will to a group of other people, much less to that group's perception of God. But that is what is required of anyone in a Hutterian community, whoever they are and however deep their faith might be. In the beginning of the Christian era, all who wanted to follow Christ sold all they had, gave the proceeds to the poor, and lived as Christ commanded.

Though this would lead to any number of interpretations in the centuries to come, this mandate guided the first Christian church community in Jerusalem in the years following the resurrection and ascension of Christ. It was a church that readers of the Bible can see described in the Book of Acts, chapters 2 and 4.

"And all that believed were together, and had all things common; and sold their possessions and goods, and parted them to all men, as every man had need. And they, continuing daily with one accord in the temple, and breaking bread from house to house, did eat their meat with gladness and singleness of heart, praising God, and having favor with all the people. And the Lord added to the church daily such as should be saved" (Acts 2:44-47, KJV).

"And the multitude of them that believed were of one heart and of one soul: neither said any of them that ought of the things which he possessed was his own; but they had all things common. And with great power gave the apostles witness of the resurrection of the Lord Jesus: and great grace was upon them all. Neither was there any among them that lacked: for as many as were possessors of land or houses sold them, and brought the price of the things that were sold, and laid them at the apostles' feet: and distribution was made unto every man according as he had need" (Acts 4:32-35, KJV).

Christ foreshadowed this church community many times in his teachings, notably in the story of the rich young ruler in the Book of Matthew, and in other references to surrender and giving up one's earthly possessions.

In Acts 5, the early believers were shown the kind of spiritual death that could be suffered by holding back from the community all that one owned, in the very real physical fate of Ananias and Sapphira. The Hutterites believe this command to surrender all did not just apply to those early days in Jerusalem, but to today's church as well. That is why the Hutterian Church has continued in this way ever since its beginning in the early 1500s, during the hardest days of the Christian Reformation in Europe.

The Hutterites say they have chosen community not only because Christ commanded it, but because they feel that it allows them to best serve one another in a Christlike way. Without the distractions of the world, and the worries of chasing money and possessions to the ends of the Earth, they feel they avoid many of the obstacles that stand between them and the God to whom they dedicate and surrender their lives.

It is only by sharing everything they have that they can bear one another's burdens, because by holding everything in common, their interests become and always remain their brother's and sister's interests as well. When all endure the same suffering, or the same joy, the thinking goes, all are equal here on Earth before one another, just as they are equal in the eyes of God.

It is a humbling life, to be in community, for the Hutterians believe they must make this surrender every day, not only when they get up in the morning but many times during the day when they might feel their old wills trying to regain them. Living in community helps to tame these inclinations, the Hutterites believe, and so they dedicate their lives and themselves to one another through work, mutual assistance, and worshipping together.

This is why the Hutterites have chosen community and why they continue to try to live it day after day, with varying degrees of success. It is a life full of struggles and agonies, and yet filled with joy and love as well, so it is not just an escape from the wickedness of the world. Nor is it utopia.

At the heart of much of the persecution the Hutterites faced during the Reformation was one tenet that they and other Anabaptist churches observe to this day. Indeed, their belief in adult or believers' baptism cost the early Hutterites dearly in bloodshed, suffering, and martyrdom.

The Hutterites believe that baptism should be given only when a person is mature and able to perceive the reality of Christ and the Holy Spirit in his or her heart. The Hutterites believe that to receive baptism, people must be converted, "born again" Christians, with peace and generosity in their hearts in keeping with Christ's teaching. In the Hutterian view of the soul, baptism marks the beginning of an arduous, lifelong commitment to Christian living, and should not be taken lightly.

Hutterites are baptized only after a period of reflection and testing, and after proving their commitment to God. As Christ did, they are urged to count the cost of joining the Christian church. And only if they are willing to accept all that will come to them, every hardship and suffering along with the joys, are they baptized and received as full members of the community.

Of course, as with any situation where human beings are involved, some who are baptized are more sincere than others. In some colonies, baptism is seen not as much as a spiritual milepost as a steppingstone to marriage, because baptism is required before a wedding can take place. This kind of spiritual dishonesty is far more prevalent than most Hutterites would care to admit, though some colonies are doing what they can to prevent this from happening.

When we lived at Starland, many of the young people, as they approached the usual age for baptism in their late teens or early 20s, seemed quite eager to express their spiritual commitments. In fact, under the influence of an evangelical "holiness" movement making its way through the colonies at that time, under the ministry of a former Amishman from Pennsylvania, several were quite zealous in desiring to be baptized.

Though some of the community leaders were pleased by this at first, others in the brotherhood were deeply troubled by the outside influences that were making themselves heard. This certainly was not the first time this had happened. The *Chronicle*, and even more recent memory, are full of such movements encroaching on the communities, and even enticing members to leave.

One spring in the late 1990s — Hutterite baptisms traditionally take place on Palm Sunday or Pentecost — a group of 12 young people of various ages decided to ask for baptism. Because some of these young adults seemed to disregard certain elements of Hutterian spirituality — especially the belief that baptism commits the person to the community for life — the colony was thrown into something of an uproar. Eventually, after several sometimes heated discussions, a few of the group of 12 were advised to wait, while the others were baptized that Palm Sunday. As it turned out, most of the original group eventually left the colony in coming years, either to live with other members of the "holiness" movement in Pennsylvania or to assimilate into the outside world.

Regarding adult baptism, it is unimaginable to the Hutterites that any infant must be baptized to receive salvation, as many churches teach. Indeed, the thinking goes, how can one without sin, or even the capability to sin, be unfit for God's love and protection? The Hutterian forefathers wrote extensively in opposition to infant baptism, and they were unshakeable in this belief, as today's Hutterites still are.

In the Hutterian Church, one can only be baptized when one is old enough and sufficiently mature to accept God. An infant is not only too immature to fully know God, but unable to offend him. When young Hutterites ask to be baptized, usually in their late teens or early 20s, they are questioned about the depth of their commitment and tested to illuminate the truth of their belief in God and Christ. It is only after this period of testing and a formal time of instruction that they confess their sins to the minister and are baptized and accepted as full members of the church community. If a person is not sure of his or her commitment, he or she is urged to wait until another time.

Many choose to take this opportunity and are typically much stronger in their faith when their baptism eventually comes. Despite the fact that some young people are baptized without any genuine maturity of faith, for most Hutterites, their baptism is perhaps the most important event in their lives. And as Christians, it is certainly central to their growth as true believers.

When a person is baptized in the Hutterian faith, he or she must agree to accept and to give correction to others in the community when it is necessary. This correction or counseling is taught in several places in the New Testament, both by Christ and later, in Paul's writings. When brothers or sisters are seen to be involved in a fault or sin, it is the responsibility of the other members in the community to approach them, privately at first, and admonish them to change. Usually this is all the counsel necessary, but if not, other steps may be taken, and if needed, the church itself will become involved. There are several degrees of this church discipline, depending on the gravity of the sin committed by the member.

At Starland, we soon saw that church discipline was not, to us anyway, the frightening penalty we had thought it might be.

To call it a "punishment" also would not be accurate by non-Hutterite standards. But to those who found themselves placed in the "*Straf*," or the "pen," as Hutterites called it — rather casually, I thought — church discipline was a major concern.

In our community, most instances of church discipline addressed relatively minor, but troubling, issues such as habitual drunkenness, smoking, leaving the colony without permission, or various interpersonal sins, such as engaging in gossip or back-stabbing. People who had been taken to task for these offenses, if they admitted their error, would then ask to be placed in church discipline. This was done at church some evening, following a brief confession by the offender.

After this confession, the minister would pronounce sentence, so to speak, usually placing the person under "avoidance," or the "*Meidung*," for a couple of weeks so they could repent of their transgressions. Because of the intense social significance this step had for most Hutterites — in essence, they were excommunicated for the duration of the *Meidung* — the offender, and sometimes others in the community, would find themselves in tears over the gravity of it all.

This avoidance usually entailed not speaking in an overly friendly manner with the person in the *Straf*, although conversations in the course of work were allowed. The offender also did not eat or attend church with the rest of the community, a measure based on various New Testament Scriptures. During church, or when mealtimes rolled around, the person under discipline usually would retreat to a room off the main church meeting place, or occasionally to the *kleine-schul*, where they could listen to the sermon or receive their meals from the kitchen in solitude.

Perhaps most grievous of all, however, was the disruption this discipline brought to the offender's marriage. At home, during the course of the *Straf*, the conjugal relationship between man and wife was suspended. With sex out the window, and with others giving them the cold shoulder, there was not much left for an offender to do but contemplate their shortcomings. Sometimes, to make the marital break even more emphatic, the wife of a male offender – and nearly all were male, in our experience – might return to her home colony for a visit during this period.

After a few weeks of avoidance, the person would be readmitted to the church in a way very similar to how they had been excluded. Following a church service, the minister would invite the offender back into the meeting room and, after another brief testimony by the one disciplined, would "speak out forgiveness," as the Hutterites say, and readmit them to the church. After this, the one just released from the *Straf* would walk around to every baptized man and woman in the room and shake hands with them – a sign regarded as one of holy reconciliation – and hear a few words of forgiveness from each one.

Though I sometimes felt that church discipline was carried out in a rather rote or superficial way, I always found this simple act of reconnecting with the community quite moving and emotional. Whenever we received someone back from the *Straf*, there was something powerful about it, especially if it seemed the discipline had done any good.

Neither Duann nor I were ever placed in discipline, though I did have to take on a much lesser penalty once. After I had received a traffic citation for not wearing a safety belt while driving, and the community had to pay a $75 fine, I was asked by the ministers to apologize during church.

Though this would seem a relatively minor matter, apologizing in such a way actually took a good deal of courage. I knew this would be the case and carried the ticket around with me for a couple of weeks as the payment deadline neared, not wanting to admit my offense until I absolutely had to. But once I had handed the ticket over to David Jr., the steward, so he could send in a check, my deed was immediately major news.

There was just something deeply humiliating, and memorable, about having to admit in front of everyone that I had transgressed the laws of the land in this foolish and cavalier manner. Looking around after my little speech of apology, I noticed that more than a few people were squelching smiles or quiet laughs, and I felt a strange silliness come over me as well.

Shifting back and forth on my feet, I realized that some were getting quite a kick out of the college-educated "world man" having to apologize for a traffic ticket. To them, I had been brought into line at last, having felt the swat of the church's authority like everyone else. I looked over at my friend Arnie Kleinsasser, the colony mechanic and blacksmith, who had an especially broad smile on his face and was nodding his head in amusement. Maybe I had been worrying about nothing, I thought. Maybe this was all a big joke.

This levity was quickly wiped away, however, when David Vetter, after speaking out my forgiveness, said, rather forcefully, "Well, that's too bad about that $75. I guess we have to pay it, though. We can't have you going to jail."

Because the community was quite wealthy, it was not the small amount of money I had cost the colony that mattered.

Instead, it was the sense that my own carelessness and inattention had somehow let the others down. To a Hutterite, for whom the communal bond is paramount, this was serious business.

Not willing to let his admonition sting too badly, though, and probably seeing the teasing smiles around the room, David Vetter added, with a chuckle of his own, "But I guess we'll let it go this time."

I have never forgotten this lesson, and I have never again failed to wear a safety belt when driving.

chapter
TWELVE

Central to life in community is also the Hutterian stance in favor of peace and nonviolence. In the Sermon on the Mount, in Matthew 5-7, Jesus taught that believers are to do no violence to anyone, and in fact, to love their enemies. The Hutterites take this to mean that they should not only abstain from violent acts against individuals, but that they should also not fight in wars or take part in civil unrest, even in self-defense. The Hutterites feel that God will protect them in times of strife and violence, and that if they are attacked, it is their perception of God's will and not theirs that should prevail.

Hutterites also refuse to swear oaths or involve themselves in the government. They do pay taxes, contrary to what some believe, because they were told to "render unto Caesar" what is his, and unto God what is God's. The Hutterites find no compromise in doing this, viewing it as an act of love to their neighbors and a way of supporting projects that many will benefit from. But their faith comes first in matters of doing violence, and so they do not involve themselves in the military or any war-related or defense-related activity, even in their business pursuits.

Before he was burned at the stake at Innsbruck, Austria, in 1536, Jakob Hutter wrote of his followers' peace convictions in a letter to the governor of Moravia. Part of this letter is preserved in the *Chronicle of the Hutterian Brethren*, published in English translation by Plough Publishing House.

"All our words and deeds, our conduct, our way of life, are there for all men to see," Hutter wrote. "Rather than knowingly wrong a man to the value of a penny, we would let ourselves be robbed of a hundred gulden. Rather than strike our worst enemy with our hand – to say nothing of spears, swords, and halberds such as the world uses – we would let our own lives be taken. As anyone can see, we have no physical weapons, neither spears nor muskets."

Over the years, Hutterites have been conscientious objectors to any military service, a status that has resulted in no small number of reprisals against them and their communities, and which has even cost lives in modern times. During World War I, four young Hutterian men were drafted and sent to the federal penitentiary at Alcatraz in San Francisco Bay. Later, in the final weeks of the war and during a nationwide influenza pandemic, they were sent by train to the U.S. Disciplinary Barracks at Fort Leavenworth, Kansas, for refusing to wear the military uniform or to do military service of any kind.

This federal prison, blazing hot in the summer and alternately cold and stultifying from steam heat in winter, was still in use as the 21st century dawned. In November 2002, when I was a journalist with *Mennonite Weekly Review*, I toured the prison with a young army sergeant who had been a guard there before the prisoners were moved to a new, state-of-the-art facility elsewhere on the base. The occasion was the prison's recent closure, and I thought at the time that on moving day, there must have been no happier group of prisoners.

In addition to the Hutterites who had died in the USDB, numerous Mennonites and members of other peace churches had been imprisoned in this jail during World War I. The rest of the time, the USDB held members of the military or other government agencies who had committed violent or subversive crimes that garnered them sentences of five years or longer. Among the prisoners when the old facility closed were turncoats who had spied for the former Soviet Union, as well as murderers and other violent offenders.

Though the Leavenworth archives make virtually no mention of the conscientious objectors held there, it is believed that quite a number of other COs also died, primarily from the influenza pandemic which struck the country in November 1918 and blazed fatally through enclosed communities such as prisons.

I stood in the narrow cells on the same block where the four Hutterites had been held – by some accounts with their hands chained to the ceiling so that their toes barely touched the concrete floor – and saw the tall, turret-like building known as "the castle," which had several wings spread out like spokes around a central hub. When we entered the building, the young sergeant unlocked the main door with a huge metal key that looked like it might have once opened some medieval brig. Inside, the stone walls held the damp chill of autumn.

The cells were about 6-by-8 feet, just deep enough for a bed and toilet and wide enough for me to spread my arms and place my hands flat against the walls. The solitary confinement cells where the Hutterites had been held seemed even more cramped in the prison's below-ground level where the boilers must have stifled the air during the cold months. In a solitary confinement cell I was shown, where inmates were kept in their underwear and manacled at all times, there was a crude shower where more violent prisoners were given what was called, not ironically, "the wire brush treatment."

This episode of confinement and torture in Alcatraz and at the USDB was perhaps the most violent result of the Hutterites' peaceful stance in modern times, but in their long history it is but a small incident in a sea of shed blood. Ever since World War II, Hutterites and other peace-witness churches, such as the Quakers, Brethren, Amish, and Mennonites, have been allowed to do alternative service in peaceful, non-military areas such as forestry and agriculture in time of war, instead of doing specifically military assignments. Most recently, this occurred during the Vietnam War, the last time there was a wartime draft. Members of these groups, along with COs who object to war on secular grounds, continue to stand up for their belief in peace, however, and continue to be criticized for it.

chapter

THIRTEEN

The grim reality of martyrdom is something the Hutterites have hard-wired in their spiritual and historical DNA, a reminder of past hardships and persecutions, and a readiness for the possibility that such fatal times might somehow return. A common sight in many *Hutterisch* homes is a large doorstop of a book called the *Martyrs Mirror*, a volume of Dutch Mennonite origins collecting stories of Christian martyrs from the time of the Apostles through the Reformation.

The first thing I noticed about the *Martyrs Mirror*, the first time I dandled a copy on my knee like a fussy child, was not its immensity. And it wasn't the ubiquitous, illustrative etchings with their merry fountains of blood, casually discarded limbs, or oddly serene-looking martyrs in the process of being crassly victimized. What I noticed was its cover – that strange, grocery-sack dust jacket that I have never seen anyplace else.

It seemed, in its unassuming plainness, to say that though this is a book afforded much respect — and possessing even a sacred resplendence — it is really only a book, made by human hands, and wrapped in whatever there was lying around to keep the elements away.

I wasn't raised as an Anabaptist, so this was my first encounter with the martyr tales of the Reformation and with the *Martyrs Mirror*. It had occurred in a rather unusual way, when I was still a secular journalist in Fayetteville, Arkansas. I had simply read about the book somewhere, and set about finding a copy, using various journalist tricks and connections to find a source.

Here is how I did it: Not far from Fayetteville, out in the Ozarks, lived a group of end-times sorts who wore shabby clothes and were very strict about photographs. We had run a story about how they resisted being photographed for their driver's licenses, and the uproar that ensued. Some said the little sect were Mennonites of some kind, though they really weren't.

I had our police reporter get me the name of their leader — I didn't mention why — and the chase was on. For a group of end-times agitators, they actually were rather helpful. They some-how could understand why a man would want to get a copy of the *Martyrs Mirror*, seemingly out of the blue, although they knew little more than I did about where to find the book.

Eventually, I bought a copy from a Holdeman Mennonite who lived nearby and sold spiritual books to the people in his conservative church, and to me, a curious newsman, who was about to begin a journey into Christian antiquity.

Thus began my own interest in the distant past of the Anabaptists. Later, in the colony, I learned the book's ponderous German title — *Der Blutige Schau-Platz oder Martyrer-Spiegel der Tauffs Gesinnten oder Wehrlosen-Christen*, roughly *The Bloody Theater of the Anabaptist Martyrs* — which the Hutterites shortened simply to *Martyrer Spiegel* in that languid way they have of shortening things.

Among mainstream Mennonites, I have heard some say that the *Martyrs Mirror*, while remaining an important historical document, no longer plays much of a role in their own spirituality. Some view it as out-of-date, a throwback to an age of pewter and Brueghel. However, among the more conservative branches of Anabaptists, most look upon the *Martyrer Spiegel* as not only vital but central to their experience as Christians.

In our community in Minnesota, it was not difficult to find a copy of the *Martyrer Spiegel*, or someone acquainted with its contents, from its accounts of horrible persecution and death to the medieval and somewhat gothic gore of Jan Luykens' engravings.

However, among the Hutterites, a similar compendium was far better known, which presented a fair complement to the *Martyrer Spiegel* and its testimonies. The *Chronicle of the Hutterian Brethren* is really two chronicles composed at different times in the Hutterian sojourn from Moravia in the 1530s to Russia in the 1700s and beyond.

The *Grosse-Geschichtbuch*, or *Great Chronicle*, is the older volume, and covers much of the same time frame as the *Martyrer Spiegel*, though with an emphasis on Hutterite martyrs, who are actually quite rare in the *Martyrs Mirror*. The *Kleine-Geschichtsbuch*, or *Small Chronicle*, condenses the history in the *Great Chronicle*, with further accounts of later centuries and migrations.

Fortunately, both volumes are now in print in English, helping guarantee their continued vitality. In our community, every home had copies of both English volumes, and among older people, the German editions as well.

The German editions seemed to be preferred more by the older people in the colony, in part because they were far more familiar with the archaic High German, which was hard for younger generations to read. I asked one of the Deckers, who was about my age, if he ever read the German *Martyrer Spiegel*, and he scratched his beard and had to admit that he didn't.

"I can't read that German," he said. "We don't really know German anymore."

Interestingly enough, the old German *fraktur* font, which resembles the elaborate Old English typefaces in some ways, posed less of a barrier than the words themselves. In church, we almost always sang German hymns from the Hutterian and Lutheran canon. Everyone was able to sing the songs, but I wondered if very many people understood the words that well. Strangely, the older High German, like that found in the hymns, was inscrutable even to actual Germans, as we learned when a family visited the colony one summer. Faced with our old-style hymns and shown a copy of Martin Luther's original German translation of the Bible, which set the standard for literary High German for centuries, these thoroughly modern Deutschlanders were unable to get very far.

"We don't understand this language," the 30-year-old husband said.

He and his wife also did not understand the Hutterian version of spoken German, either, much less *Hutterisch*, although the wife, being from Tyrol, could make out some of the Hutterian dialect. Ultimately, she found it too complicated with its additions of Russian and English words and phrases. Before long, the Hutterites and the Germans found it best to speak to one another in English, another concession to the modern world and its encroachments.

This language gap also proved rather embarrassing in our dealings with this family, who were very earnest seekers, looking for a different way to express their faith in their daily lives. The day after the couple and their children arrived from the Minneapolis airport, some of the colony members were standing around in our front yard following Sunday *Lehr*.

The visitors were there, too, chased from their guesthouse by the lack of air-conditioning on this hot summer afternoon. As Hutterite men are wont to do, Clarence Wollman complimented the visiting German on his wife, whom he referred to as a "*Weib*," which in German truly does mean "wife." Almost immediately, though, it became obvious that the wife in question was deeply offended by this "compliment," which also seemed to leave her husband a bit baffled.

"What? What?" Clarence asked. "What did I say?"

It turned out that "*Weib*," in modern German usage, was a euphemism for "prostitute." Real Germans, we realized, employed the very common term "*Frau*" when referring to their proper and upright wives.

This misunderstanding was smoothed over quickly enough, but it must have seemed to that family that our community was crawling with women of ill repute. That summer, over the colony public-address system, David Vetter would call the "*Weibe und Diene*," the "wives and girls," to the garden for the usual weeding and hoeing. Often, he modified this to "*Schwestern und Diene*," or "sisters and girls," and sometimes, after all the confusion had ensued, he simply issued his call in unmistakable English. But the trouble did not stop there. When the gardeners were summoned to the main yard, they boarded a tractor-drawn vehicle known around the colony as the "wife wagon," which carried not only the gardeners but their hoes and spades and other implements out to the rows of sweet corn and beans. In *Hutterisch*, this conveyance was referred to just as often as the "*Weibewog*," or, in the modern German usage we had no idea of, the "prostitute wagon."

It must have seemed to that poor woman, who found herself adrift among a community of Russo-German peasants for a big chunk of the summer, that our place was not only home to a klatch of streetwalkers, but that we had built a special wagon to haul them around!

Apparently our visitors were none too perturbed, however. This family, which eventually added two more children, came back for more visits over the years and became almost *de facto* members of the community. Whenever colony members traveled to Europe on business, they would stop and visit this family and often took them along on their motor and train jaunts around the continent.

Language was a stumbling block in other ways. Back in South Dakota, a Kentucky-bred junk dealer named Paul Ponder used to make the rounds, hitting all the Dakota colonies, including Pembrook Colony, Starland's parent community, with his serendipitous array of wares and appliances. One day, Paul Ponder pulled up in his truck and asked outright if Pembrook's denizens could use an "ass machine." The men he was talking to all looked at one another and shook their heads, puzzled, not comprehending what they were being offered.

"A *what?*" one of them asked.

"Ass machine. You know, an *ass machine*. Makes ass. It's good ass, too."

Looking at the ramshackle device Paul Ponder was pointing at, everyone slowly caught on that what he was hawking was an ice-maker.

"Oh, an *ice machine*," one of the men blustered.

"Rat, rat. An ass machine. Makes good ass. You want it?"

Apparently they did not, but Paul Ponder and his broad Kentucky vowels were the sources of much levity for years to come. This story always came up whenever my own Southern accent left someone confused.

"You sound just like Paul Ponder," I was told more than once. "Robert Vetter, you want to buy an *ass machine*?"

~

Traditionally, when Hutterites are married, they receive from the colony not an ice machine but a family Bible, the two *Chronicles*, and an equally immense book of 400-year-old Hutterian hymns, many of them martyr stories composed by early Hutterites imprisoned in dank Reformation dungeons, sometimes before being martyred themselves.

Though anyone would admit that none of us were of the same spirit and mettle as the early Hutterians, the accounts of their lives and deaths provided us a kind of moral guardian and lent a certain authenticity to our continued experience as communal Christians.

Consider that until the early 20th century, both Hutterian *Chronicles* existed only in handwritten form, in volumes of archaic German passed down amid fire and persecution and flight, miraculously preserved. This is how important those books and their contents were and are today.

One of these handwritten volumes, a copy of the *Great Chronicle* dating to 1581, resides with other handwritten books in the minister's home at Bonhomme Colony, the first North American colony, established in 1874 when the Hutterites migrated to the United States from Ukraine. Built atop a cliff overlooking the Missouri River near Tabor, South Dakota, Bonhomme is still a very traditional colony, observant of many of the old Hutterian practices and prohibitions that other communities have long given up.

When I visited there in the late 1990s and saw the *Great Chronicle*, a privilege I had looked forward to, I was quite astonished and stunned by what I saw. The handwritten volume, which was used by early 20th century Hutterite minister Elias Walter to produce and modernize the High German of the *Chronicle*'s first printed edition, published in Vienna in 1923, was kept in a large wooden box and slid beneath the bed of the colony's elderly minister, Jakob Waldner. Some shreds of old transatlantic mailing labels, some in Elias Walter's calligraphic hand, showed the box had been used to ship the book's rewritten manuscript to Austria before becoming the repository of the antique original. Hutterite thrift at work!

White of beard and weak in the eyes in keeping with his advanced years, Waldner had the look and bearing of an Old Testament prophet, but dressed in black and suspenders instead of a desert tunic. One Hutterite friend of mine, Dave Wurz, who was then in his 50s and had been born at Bonhomme before moving to a branch colony farther west as a child, said Waldner had always cut a rather biblical-looking figure. "Jake Vetter looked old *when I was a kid*," he said.

One Sunday afternoon, when Waldner had risen from his Sabbath nap, I was ushered into his comfortable and orderly study, where the minister regularly held court and showed the *Chronicle* to all who came. Though I knew the book was an antiquity, its condition was appalling. The age-old calf vellum pages had long ago discolored and even begun to mildew in places, due no doubt to the humidity that regularly hangs over this riverside colony.

On that afternoon, in early summer, the damp heat was sweltering and the book's pages – which, after all, had once been the skin of a living, medieval bovine – literally seemed to sweat with moisture. On many pages, the 400-year-old ink had either begun to fade or had eaten through the vellum, and other leaves were horribly brittle and beginning to disintegrate, probably due to all the handling the book had received over the centuries.

Slowly and tenderly, Waldner turned a few of the sturdier pages and showed me some of the volume's archaic, occasionally ornate penmanship before returning the book to its box and its place beneath his bed.

Though scholars have been welcomed to make off-site microfilms of the entire volume, which comprises 612 folio-size pages and is quite rich in some of its decorative illustrations, others have bemoaned the volume's treatment and the fact that it is not kept in a climate-controlled archive.

When fire demolished Waldner's former house, one of the colony's oldest cliff-chalk structures, the *Chronicle* and some of the colony's other handwritten treasures were rescued unscathed. Later, a more modern house was constructed with somewhat better conditions, in part to help preserve the Hutterians' fragile corpus of faith, but also to make its ancient minister a bit more comfortable in his waning years.

Still, despite the addition of air-conditioning and controlled central heat – luxuries not then available in other colony residences at Bonhomme – the *Chronicle* is still an endangered treasure, a reality that scholars, and other Hutterites, have come to grudgingly accept.

Bonhomme's ancient cliffs protect it from seasonal floods. Those tend to flow into a manmade lake in neighboring Nebraska, into an area known as the Devil's Nest, where Jesse James was said to have hidden out.

Still, there is always the risk of fire – long a Hutterian nemesis that demolished entire colonies back in the 1600s – someday claiming the *Chronicle*, as it nearly did several times over the book's history. According to old accounts, these fires tended to strike amid the snowy glimmer of deep winter, allowing the cold to claim even more lives, usually those of children.

Then there is the greatest threat of all on the Plains – tornadoes – to contend with. More than once, spring twisters have skirted the colony without actually striking it. Waldner told me that even while he depends on his faith to protect the *Chronicle* – a task he has carried out with great humility since being made its custodian – he frequently has imagined scenarios of its destruction.

A tornado sweeping it away, he said, makes him most nervous of all. On the rainy evening I was in his home, the sky briefly turned a bilious green, and Waldner's eyes darted periodically to a nearby window, drawn by several low rumbles of thunder. When the weather eventually cleared, with only a momentary downpour to mark its passing and freshen the air, the old minister seemed relieved.

Though it might be possible to convince the colony to surrender the *Chronicle* for restoration and safekeeping, keeping the volume in Hutterian hands also seems proper and even imperative. That the book has survived this long, and is still accorded such reverence by the nearly 50,000 Hutterites in communities today, is testament to its continued vitality and importance to a living people. Making it a museum piece would seem, in one way, to defy this currency and estrange the book from today's Hutterian worldview. Still, restoring and preserving the book would ensure its availability as a witness to a brutal past for generations to come.

A few hundred miles away from Bonhomme, near St. Cloud, Minnesota, is a place where the *Chronicle* easily could receive the treatment it deserves. The Hill Monastic Manuscript Library, on the grounds of St. John's Abbey, a large Benedictine monastery that also hosts a men's university, is one of the world's biggest repositories of illuminated manuscripts, some more recent than the *Chronicle*.

Somehow, though, entrusting the *Chronicle* — with all its stories of persecution and murder committed by the Catholic Church — to a Catholic institution would present an irony even the most liberal Hutterite would have a hard time accepting. I would, and I was probably about as liberal as they came.

And so even now, the centuries-old *Chronicle* remains where it has for nearly 150 years — under a bed in a minister's house on the banks of the Missouri River. I find it usually serves me best not to worry about the fate of this old book, trusting that somehow it will endure, perhaps even longer than the Hutterites themselves.

∼

The *Chronicle* is not the only ready source of Hutterite history. There is another supply of Hutterian martyr stories as well, a selection of *Hutterisch episteln* or letters written by early

Hutterite leaders. These were some of the most heartfelt and heartbreaking of all testimonies – composed in the moment, written in blood and with the shadows of strife and starvation close by.

I remember during *Gebet* one winter evening at Starland – with frost on the schoolhouse windows and a forlorn gibbous moon rising above our corner of the prairie – hearing David Vetter read such a letter from Jakob Hutter, not long before Hutter was burned at the stake in Innsbruck in 1536.

Hutter had exiled himself from the community in Tyrol, in part to protect others in the church from his pursuers. Some Hutterites have speculated that his surname was even an alias, necessitated by nearly three years of flight and in keeping with his work as a hatmaker. In his letters back to Tyrol, he wrote of living out on the heath with a group of other followers, exposed to the elements, not knowing if he would live to write again.

So often these letters, written initially by Hutter and later by others, would include a kind of appeal universal to this sort of writing, and that to many Hutterites still presents a call to faithfulness. "Remember me," these refugees would write. "Remember me to the brothers and sisters, to the elders and the other servants, to young and old, and beg their forgiveness for my shortcomings."

Usually these letters would end with a call to keep the church together as long as possible, and the final hope that in heaven, all would be reunited and the tears of those bitter days forgotten.

In 1533, Hutter wrote a long, pleading letter to the church community in Tyrol. This letter embodies in many ways the cold suffering of the times. Hutter wrote at once of the immense, reassuring joy his faith brought him and others in the church.

Then, a few lines later, he expressed deep concern for the lives of the people in the community, who daily faced the risk of arrest, torture, and execution.

"There is great fear and anxiety in our hearts on your account, and we find no rest by day or by night (God is our witness in this and in all things) because you are being persecuted and tortured with utmost cruelty and secretly murdered or suppressed. May God in heaven have mercy! It wounds our hearts to the quick that you are being taken from us like this. ... In conclusion, I commend all of you to the protection of God's mighty hand. May the Lord be your guard and captain, your shelter and shield, keeping safe your souls and bodies until the great day of the Lord's revelation, through Jesus Christ."

In 1535, Hutter wrote another letter to the Moravian governor, this one from out on the heath where he and some other followers had fled and were barely surviving. This was the letter we heard during *Gebet* that night.

"It does not trouble us that many evil things are said about us, for Christ foretold all this. ... You fear a weak, mortal man more than the living, eternal, almighty God and are willing to expel and ruthlessly persecute the children of God, old and young, even the Lord's widows and orphans in their need and sorrow, and deliver them up to plunder, fear, great suffering, and extreme poverty. It is as if you strangled them with your own hands. We would rather be murdered for the Lord's sake than witness such misery inflicted on innocent, God-fearing hearts. You will have to pay dearly for it, and you will have no more excuse than Pilate."

It was such a profound experience to listen to letters such as this, all of us crowded into our church room in the school, the blacksmith next to the farm boss, in our dusty black clothes at the end of another day. David Vetter's voice, though never terribly loud or emphatic, was unusually quiet and fragile when he read this, as if the essence of the suffering experienced by his Hutterian ancestors had been inherited and replicated even among us in our safe and prosperous commune. I have never forgotten it.

Afterward, stepping into the frozen night, with only the empty fields for miles around, I glimpsed for a moment the loneliness of such unthinkable sorrow, and the collective past shared by these people I lived with became real in a way it never had. For a moment, I could sense the reality of the sadness and detachment many of them still felt, even if they couldn't name or understand it themselves.

$$\sim$$

Yet another corpus of literature also has been passed down by the Hutterites — a collection of sermons that traditionally have been handwritten by or for succeeding ministers and handed from one generation to the next. In many ways, this slow, intensive task, which could take years to complete, was the closest parallel to theological training that a minister would receive.

This practice, made nearly obsolete today by cheap and highly legible digital printing, also helped preserve among the Hutterites the art of bookbinding, with many colonies once maintaining their own binderies, or supporting another colony's binding works.

In Starland, David Vetter had a large collection of old sermon books, copied by both him and his father, who also had been a minister, many of them bound in supple maroon-colored leather. Some volumes in David Vetter's possession were copied by a female relative, who apparently was enthusiastic about copying sermons but was known for making numerous mistakes. David Vetter said he had simply learned to read around these "typos" whenever they cropped up.

The sermons were copied out, in German of course, in what the Hutterites call *sütterlin* script, an angular, cursive hand that resembles but does not replicate *Latinische*, or Roman, script.

Today, Hutterites are probably among the few, if not the only, practitioners of *sütterlinschrift* in the world, although its use is starting to die out in less traditional colonies. To the unaccustomed eye, it is certainly much harder to read than standard Western cursive writing. There also is a great deal of variety in the *sütterlin* style used by the various Hutterian *leut*.

While the Schmied *sütterlin* has broader, thicker lines, the style used by the Lehrerleut, who still emphasize the copying of sermons by new ministers, is much more angular and precise, giving the impression of having been written with a steel-nibbed pen such as cartographers once used. In recent years, computer-based *sütterlin* fonts have been developed and even come into use among some Hutterites, though more seem to prefer typical Roman or *fraktur* fonts for the reproduction of sermons and hymns.

These Hutterian sermons, of which about 300 or more are said to exist, are divided into two groups – *Lehren*, or full-length sermons, and *Vorreden*, or prefatory sermons that precede the main sermon during a Sunday or holiday service. While the shorter *Vorreden* tend to address subjects more generally, the *Lehren* are structured discourses based on specific biblical texts.

Typically, these texts are taken verse by verse and flossed out, sometimes at great length. Some *Lehren* are short enough to be read in their entirety during a single service, while some are broken up and continued during weeknight *Gebet* services. Sermons specific to church holidays such as Christmas, Easter, and Pentecost are read in their season, as are sermons related to church ordinances such as baptism, the Lord's Supper, weddings, and funerals.

In Starland, we were summoned to church — first in our school and later, once it was completed, in a large room next to the dining hall in the communal kitchen — by a tone broadcast over the colony PA system. I always found this raucous, artificial sound annoying, a far cry from the old brass bell that called us to meals and other activities when we first lived in the community.

Somehow, the bell, which eventually became obsolete as the colony outgrew the reach of its sound, seemed vaguely traditional and correct in its simplicity. Today it sits out in one of the colony yards, down the hill from the kitchen, surrounded in the warm months by a rose bower, a decorative, perhaps even vaguely quaint, relic of the near past.

In church, we sat with our spouses and older children, a departure from typical Hutterite practice, in which the men and women sit on opposite sides of the room in order of age, with the youngest at the front. Traditionally, the ministers and witness brothers sit on a bench at the front of the room, facing the congregation. Instead of this regimented order, however, we Starlanders sat in a rather higgledy-piggledy fashion, wherever we wanted.

This seemed to me to afford a kind of equality not always seen in other communities. It also mixed up the ranks and social strata of the colony beyond age or seniority, putting shop workers or teachers next to the blacksmith or the farm boss.

During evening *Gebet* services, a collective sense of exhaustion sometimes pervaded the room, especially on summer days when the few weeks of heat we experienced took a special toll on everyone. In winter, we all seemed particularly quiet, as if the deadening cold we had passed through to get to the church room precluded any sense of festivity. We brought the cold in with us, but gradually, a gentle warming seemed to set in – as much a spiritual reality as a physical state.

Once everyone was seated, the minister leading the service would always start – sometimes in German, sometimes in English – "Let us begin in the name of God," which in *Hutterisch* sounded like little more than *"In Gottes Nomen."* We then would sing about a dozen verses of a hymn, followed by a short sermon during *Gebet*, or a *Vorreden* during Sunday *Lehr*.

During *Gebet*, the short sermon would be followed by a communal prayer, then another hymn and a brief benediction. During *Lehr*, the *Vorreden* would be followed by a prayer, then by the longer main sermon, the actual *Lehr* itself. After this sermon, we would sing another hymn and were then dismissed with a brief benediction, as during *Gebet*.

All told, our *Gebet* services lasted perhaps a half hour, while *Lehr* lasted perhaps 75 minutes. In other colonies, especially those that held to more traditional practices, *Lehr* would be considerably longer, though the typical use of pews or chairs for church services offered a little comfort. At some point, the leaders of Starland had decided that making a church service into a feat of endurance favored neither the bodies nor the spirits of those compelled to endure it.

On the other hand, like services in all colonies, ours could still seem formulaic and even rote, especially the communal prayer, which seldom varied beyond a few minor changes here and there, or an occasional special petition. The only time I can recall a special prayer being offered during this time was the day of the September 11, 2001, terrorist attacks, which seemed to strike the colony people with as much grief and astonishment as the rest of the country.

Some Hutterites who had sat through these services most of their lives found them boring and unfulfilling. Others, however, such as me, still saw their more enlightening aspects, though after a few years, I did tense up when certain parts seemed mindlessly plain and empty. At the heart of this kind of contention were the sermons themselves.

The practice of reading prewritten sermons, many of them thought to be more than 300 years old, is one of the more controversial and least understood of Hutterian traditions. On the face of it, hearing the same cycle of sermons over and over again would seem not only boring but spiritually irrelevant to most people, including some Hutterites. Others, however, believe these tested and carefully preserved writings present the ultimate in spiritual safety, allowing no room for dangerous innovation.

In practice, however, it is not this clear-cut. In some colonies, and probably in a growing number of Hutterian communities, an experienced minister might start by reading from a sermon, and then branch off with his own words, though seldom straying from the themes or ideas at hand.

In other colonies, a minister might slavishly adhere to the written text, seldom trying to insert more than a word or two of his own, and this only sparingly and never to the extent that controversy might be introduced.

In Starland, the emerging trend of having sermons in English began about the time of our arrival, necessitated in part by our being English speakers, but also by the simple fact that many younger Hutterites do not understand the High German the sermons are composed in.

Because we spoke only English, it took a fair amount of time and effort for our family to acclimate to the *Hutterisch* dialect. This led to some feelings of isolation at first. With time, we all became fluent in at least comprehending *Hutterisch*, as well as much of the High German, though Duann and I never spoke more than a few phrases or sentences that were not English in our daily conversation. Our children, of course, learned *Hutterisch* very quickly, as children often do with new languages, and eventually were fluent in High German as well, speaking English with heavy Hutterian accents that they did not shed for several years after we left the colony.

For a good part of the time we were at Starland, I was asked to help with the editing and printing of English language sermons and prefaces, a process that continued after we left. For me, a non-minister, and an outsider at that, to be entrusted with this kind of work was extremely unorthodox.

However, because I was a writer, and because few others had the inclination to do this sort of work, my involvement was generally accepted, and I officially was given time to pursue it. At a certain point, this work came to be expected of me, and it became a part of my identity in the community, with people joking that I should "run for minister" when an opening came up — something I found not the least bit attractive.

Traditionally, newly elected ministers soon began copying their own set of sermons, a process that might take years and require borrowing various texts from ministers in other colonies. Typically, this work occurred at night or during long stretches of winter seclusion, with the minister working at his desk with a fountain pen, bent over the lined bundles of paper signatures that, once filled, would be bound into hardback volumes, sometimes by the minister himself.

This act of copying, painstakingly and for many hours at a time, was a form of liturgical and theological training for the new pastor, offering some of the spiritual education that a "worldly" minister might receive in a seminary or university. By poring over this corpus of old writing, all of it biblically based and adherent to traditional Anabaptist teaching, the minister's hands and eyes and memory became imbued, after a fashion, with the essence of Hutterian communalism.

It is true that listening to some of these sermons, even when the language was comprehensible, could be as dull as it was enlightening. Simply put, some of the sermons are much better than the others, usually those that were forged in the midst of great persecution, when the early Hutterites were literally, at times, aflame for their faith.

David Wollman, a minister at Neuhof Colony about 80 miles south of Starland, told me once, in the Hutterites' naturally ironic way, that "our sermons are so beautiful because they are written in blood."

Indeed, some of them are quite beautiful, evocative of a faith and shared experience that most churches have no concept of in the modern age. But even the most beautiful and eloquent sermon, if it is spoken without conviction or by someone who does not even understand it, can be worse than dull. Such inept spiritual teaching can be dangerously misleading, and the Hutterites are instinctively aware of this.

chapter
FOURTEEN

Nightwatch, 2 a.m.

From the old kitchen, I step across the gravel drive to the large, two-story school building which houses multi-grade classrooms for grades K-8, as well as an apartment for the schoolmaster, Joel Decker, his wife, Becky, and their six children. There is seldom much to check in this building, because Joel usually makes sure that all the lights are off and everything else is squared away.

When we first moved to the colony, the church room was also on the ground floor of this building, but has since been moved to adjoin the new dining room on the colony's south side. The school also houses the colony library, which was actually very well-stocked as colony libraries go. For a long time after we moved here, I seldom went into the library, because of the frisson of guilt, or perhaps it was a kind of homesickness, it gave me. Having left behind the literary life, it was painful to dally with it even casually. Eventually, I overcame this, and my literary interests resumed at full intensity, especially after I was asked to take up work on the sermon translations, and I started writing about the colony and related issues in various magazines.

~

One part of my writing life that I did not take up again in the colony was poetry, which had been my main pursuit in college and for a long time after. After years as a newspaper journalist, I had come to focus almost exclusively on nonfiction writing, although I did write a few pieces of fiction, in which I explored the lives of the hunters and farmers I grew up around. Even after I started writing and publishing verse again, in 2002, I have only written once about the Hutterites in this manner. For whatever reason, when it comes to our time in the colony, I haven't felt that tingle of intrigue that often precedes a poem. This single poem, which could be read as critical of the Hutterian propensity for alcohol abuse as much as an observational piece about the prairie, appeared in a chapbook of mine, *Crows Mouth*, published in Kansas in 2007.

Frank Fools Crow, who died in 1989, was a well-known Lakota medicine man who lived on the Pine Ridge reservation in western South Dakota. Whether he ever had any interaction with the Hutterites I have no idea. Either way, he represents for me, as for many, something of the prairie's native faith and the struggle for survival of all the people on the Plains.

Fools Crow: Hutterites:
April 2005

In Sisseton, South Dakota,
Hutterites line up like gingham crows
for doctor appointments every Thursday:
mostly girls, old women and the men
who drive them to town.
The men go for whiskey
or tractor parts or both
while they wait to collect
the women and stop last of all
at the pharmacy where
the charge account is.

In Sisseton, South Dakota, the ghost
of a Lakota medicine man,
Frank Fools Crow, watches the Hutterites
and the Indians file out from the liquor store.
Sitting in his pickup,
invisible to this night-turning world,
he makes his willow stick prayer
to end all war,
to end all car wrecks
on the Pine Ridge road,
to end all drunken self-destruction that even
the sundance cannot atone.
The Hutterites,
knowing nothing of ghosts anymore,
head back to their dirt-road communes,
peasants after a fashion who

have forgotten who they are,
much less who they were.

Fools Crow prays,
face like old cottonwood bark,
hewn by a century's hard resplendent wind.

Twilight, or its
cloud-feathered accomplice,
settles in the west.

~

During our years in the community, I continued to read quite widely, still focusing on nonfiction as I had when I was a journalist, but gradually veering back into modern fiction and philosophy. The plethora of libraries and college bookstores in the Twin Cities and St. Cloud – where I became a regular at the extremely well-stocked bookstore at the large Benedictine school, St. John's University – made this pursuit of variety possible.

Of course, few others in the community shared these enthusiasms, and some even called them into question. Still, enough people, such as David Vetter, the minister, shared my interests that they were tolerated and even encouraged to a degree because they fed my various intellectual appetites and "kept me off the streets," so to speak.

Of course, I also came close to running afoul of colony practice a few times because of this. In 2001, when the well-received movie *Iris* came out, I decided that I would break ranks for an afternoon and go see it. The film, recounting the life of Irish novelist and philosopher Iris Murdoch, starred Kate Winslet and Judi Dench and was showing at a theater in St. Paul.

Iris Murdoch had been one of my favorite authors since high school, and I felt that taking this liberty of going to "the cinema," as Hutterites called such worldly amusements, would not hurt me that much. After all, I reasoned, others in the colony went to fairs, rodeos, and even tractor pulls, events I found not only unappealing but bizarre.

Our minister, David Vetter, told me once that when he was a child, growing up at Barrickman Colony in Manitoba, he sometimes sneaked into movies when he accompanied some of the men to town on errands. His favorite movie star, he said, was Claudette Colbert, the French actress. Years later, he recalled her exotic accent and said she seemed very beautiful to a young boy used to seeing only hard-working Hutterite women.

In town for a medical appointment, I bought a ticket for a 2:30 p.m. showing of *Iris*, which would allow me to get home at a decent hour without anyone being the wiser. I took my seat, ready to watch the first movie I had been to see in nearly 20 years, as it turned out. Though I knew that, strictly speaking, I was not supposed to be there, I ignored the cloying Greek chorus in my head, wailing my certain doom for using the collective's money to clutter my mind with distracting images of Kate Winslet. My Hollywood escapade would not last long, however.

About five minutes into the film, the computer hard-drive that projected the movie apparently crashed, immersing the theater in sudden darkness. After a few moments, the house lights came back on. As I sat there blinking, a voice announced that this showing of the film had been cancelled and that our money would be refunded.

Taking this as something of a sign, and unwilling to wait until the 5:30 show when I figured the roof might actually cave in, I left.

~

After leaving the school, I drive back to the far south end of the colony, to check the last major building of the night, the large, two-story kitchen and storage building that sits atop a shallow hill overlooking the rest of the community. This building was completed a year or two after we had arrived in the colony and included not only the kitchen and dining room, but the church room, the kleine-schul, and a number of large food and equipment storage areas, as well as a fully-equipped industrial laundry. Like most colony structures, it was entirely Hutterite-built, even down to the stainless steel kitchen counters and a hydraulic freight elevator, all of which Arnie Kleinsasser built in his blacksmith's shop.

Whenever I was on nightwatch, it was always the kitchen I looked over the closest. Something, somewhere, was always left on, sometimes at great risk, or sometimes because of some frustrating degree of carelessness I detected in some people in the colony. The first place I checked was always the big ranges and cooking grills, which quite often had a unit still burning for some reason. Occasionally, I began to wonder if someone left these units going just to test the watchman. Other times, there would be a whiff of gas in the air, and if it lingered, I would call Conrad, who would come and check it out.

*After sticking my head into the large walk-in freezer and
refrigerator, I passed through the laundry, where there was
usually a load of wash going even late at night, and then to
the church room, where a quick pass of the flashlight always
revealed nothing out of the ordinary.*

～

If the colony could be said to have a spiritual center, in
many ways it was this room where our frequent church services brought us all together, not only in prayer, but to make
important decisions or solve serious problems in the community. During our time in the colony, two of the most serious
problems we tackled in this room was the abuse of alcohol
among a handful of colony members, and the ongoing conflict
between the Hutterian Church and the Bruderhof Communities, now known as Church Communities International, a
communal group with German roots that for many years was
aligned with the Hutterites.

Because the Hutterites have always allowed some degree of
alcohol use, some colonies to a greater extent than others, alco-
holism always has been an issue. Whether this was addressed
depended on the members and leadership of the community
in question, and how serious they were about dealing with this
illness among them. Because I had been a drunk for many years
myself, I was opposed to any habitual alcohol abuse and did not
drink often myself, other than an occasional can of cold beer
at supper on a hot day. Most others, though, did not share this
experience or outlook, and tragically, this led to a few people
becoming dependent on liquor, usually whiskey or gin or vodka
of some sort. In Starland we dealt with this issue with rather

mixed success, but at least we attempted to bring it out into the open. I finally realized that this was not a problem I was going to solve on my own, and that we could either live with it or not.

The Bruderhof issue was an entirely different matter, however, and probably unleashed more discontent and upset on our community than anything else during our time there. It also probably contributed the most to our eventual departure.

Founded amid the idealistic German youth movement of the 1920s, the Bruderhof started as a Christian communal group that patterned itself very closely on the Hutterites of old. When its earnest and idealistic founder, Eberhard Arnold, learned there were still Hutterites in North America, he undertook a journey of more than a year to visit all the colonies and seek to unite his small group with the Hutterian Church. This eventually was done, and in 1930, Arnold was baptized and ordained as a minister during a ceremony at Standoff Colony, a Dariusleut community in Alberta led by influential elder Elias Walter, who had ushered the Hutterian *Chronicles* and other old documents into print years before. Though the relationship between the German Hutterites and their traditional counterparts remained distant, mostly because of geography, it became quite strained when the Bruderhof had to flee Hitler's Germany, first to Liechtenstein, then Great Britain, then Paraguay, where the strain and estrangement between the two groups only grew.

This led to an all-out rupture between the groups in the 1950s, when the Bruderhof began establishing communities in the United States and the differences between the groups could no longer be overlooked. A reuniting between the churches came about in 1974, which led to close relations for several years. But by the early 1990s, the strains had returned in full force, and a new rupture, this one probably permanent, occurred.

This impacted Starland in part because our community had been one of the western Hutterite colonies to harbor close ties to the Bruderhof. Many people at Starland had spent time in Bruderhof settlements and had found the spiritual life there superior to the more traditional colonies in the West. Others, ethnic Hutterites, had married into Bruderhof families, which included quite a number of new converts during the 1980s. This break with the Bruderhof created immense strife in Starland, because it left those wanting to support the Bruderhof at odds with their fellow community members, who also happened to be their relatives in most cases.

This fracture also made life for us rather complicated, because it meant people on both sides of the issue tended to question our presence there. The more traditional Hutterites who opposed the presence of "outsiders" in their colonies viewed us in one way, while the Bruderhof supporters tended to question why we would want to come to such a place to begin with. The thinking among these people was that if we could find a place in what they viewed as a corrupt, spiritually empty place, then we couldn't be worth having around anyway.

Though most people in Starland were not inclined this way, we know there were a few aligned with the Bruderhof who had intentionally sought to undermine our presence there. And when they couldn't do that, they simply alienated us personally, especially Duann, who as a woman was an easy target. This was probably the most frustrating part of our six years in the community, and also one of the biggest reminders that this place was no utopia. Nevertheless, as strangers who had insinuated themselves into this place, we found the family spats and struggles as troubling and divisive as anything else we encountered. In the end, we knew this would be why we would leave.

Still, the church room was the place of many fond memories for us. On Sunday, December 7, 1997, this was the place where we had become formal members of the community and where, minutes later, our wedding vows were renewed in the Hutterian Church. When Duann and I had eloped and been married, it had been a civil ceremony carried out by a judge.

Duann had always wanted a church wedding, however, and though this was not required of us in the community, when David Vetter offered to marry us again, we accepted. Following this, the community, as a surprise to Duann, gave us a traditional Hutterite wedding celebration, complete with decorations, a big cake, and a large meal in the dining room. After this ensued a long afternoon of singing and celebration, which was attended by people from several colonies, including many of our friends from Canadian communities.

Looking back on our years in Starland, this single day stands out to me as one of the most memorable and holds the fondest sentiments for both of us.

~

After passing through the lower floor of the kitchen, mostly empty other than the kleine-schul and Josh Vetter's large, well-stocked shoe room, where most of the colony members receive new footwear of nearly every imaginable kind, I am mostly finished with the building watch. Driving back into the main yard, I check a few other smaller outbuildings, including the new pole barn where the horses are kept and where Conrad occasionally leaves a light or two on.

Our daughter Shelby tended to give this barn a wide berth after being chased by an exuberant rooster there once. When she was four or five, Shelby's long red braids had attracted the attention of a snow-white rooster named Baker, apparently because his feathers resembled baking flour. Running away only caused the rooster to flap and spur even more, and soon his claws nearly became entangled in Shelby's thick braids. It was then that Shelby had the idea of jumping on her bicycle, which still had training wheels, to speed her escape. This maneuver, of course, had the opposite effect, and just as Baker was about to dig into her hair, Conrad came running across the yard and tossed the rooster back in his pen. Shelby always recalls with considerable glee that Baker was soon murdered by a fox that crept into his habitat one night, a form of natural reckoning that farm children often regard as a breed of retribution.

Now nearly 16, Shelby still talks about this narrow brush with violence and still avoids living poultry whenever she can. Shelby remembers more fondly the experiences she and the other children had, such as working with the women in the large communal garden, going out to pick rhubarb and chamomile, and especially horseback-riding, a skill she carried with her to Kansas, where she frequently won ribbons and trophies in 4-H equine competitions.

Leaving the pole barn, which is dark and silent tonight, I drive toward another, much older barn that must have been on the original place when the colony members bought it in the mid-1980s. This old barn, with a broad, rounded roof like those seen on many Minnesota farms, has an old woodstove that *sometimes needs to be stoked during the winter, especially if any baby chicks or other animals are being cared for there. At times, a small egg-laying operation was set up in the back of the barn as well.*

Following this, the watchman is left pretty much to his own designs, making an occasional pass through the yard — in the truck during winter or on foot when it is warm — and watching for anything or anyone unusual to come along. This is especially necessary during the snowy months, when some of our farm neighbors, such as the families who live on some of the smaller acreages we own close by, or people who get lost in a white-out, might slide into a ditch and become stranded.

More than once, the colony watchman has helped a motorist in the snow, and, during blizzards, used the colony bulldozer to keep the road passable, at least as far as our closest neighbor's place, for most of the night.

During the warmer months, especially in summer, I might drive the section of property our homeplace sat on, encompassing several hundred acres of corn or soybeans. During these ventures, skunks were a common sight, bounding out of the corn into the midnight air and passing through the watch truck's headlights. Several times I came close to hitting one of these silent, ambling creatures as it emerged from the darkness, and one night, nearly walked straight into one as it lingered near the foot of our sidewalk at home.

After making my final pass through the yard, sometime between 3 and 4 a.m., the high beams strobing the barns and windows and telephone poles, I usually went back to my house and lay down on our living room couch, where I often drifted off to sleep with my heavy coat and boots still on. Though strictly speaking, I was still responsible to keep an eye on things, I always told myself I would be instantly alert if anything amiss should happen out in the yard someplace.

Nothing ever did, or at least I never heard about it.

chapter
FIFTEEN

The spring after we arrived in Starland, we saw the community put to one of the hardest tests of its life — a disaster that exacted a high enough cost as it was, but that could have destroyed the entire colony and everyone in it.

On the afternoon of Saturday, May 18, 1996, a hot and extremely humid day, we closed the shop at noon when the shop foremen decided to take all of us on a fishing trip to the Crow River in Hutchinson. I had just started my work as a welder a month or two before and was still rather enthusiastic about my success in this new area of my livelihood.

Instead of going to lunch that day, I remained at my welding table, trying to finish an order of parts that needed to be welded for a colony in Manitoba. Though I was scolded later for breaking ranks like this, the few skills I possessed in this department would soon turn out to be fortuitous.

After the usual Saturday *mittag* of *klops*, or hamburgers, eaten on fresh Saturday buns (something of a universal practice among Schmied colonies) about 20 of us — including several teenagers who wanted to come along — gathered our fishing equipment and met at the colony bus, which had been parked in the yard in front of our house. I had never been fishing in the colony before, so I was given a spare spinning rod by Sam and a plastic, pocket-sized tackle box like one I had used years before on the Dean's Island chute. Equipped with this and my standard-issue Hutterite box-cutter, I was ready to go.

One of the first tasks after we reached town was to purchase a fishing license for me and for the other colony members whose licenses had lapsed since the year before. In the bait shop where we bought our permits, it was decided that it would be cheaper if I pretended to be married to one of the colony girls so we could get a family discount, saving the community perhaps an entire dollar.

I just shook my head and acceded, seeing this as another instance of typical Hutterite reasoning, the contradictions of which I was slowly growing accustomed to. I could tell, though, that Helena, my dark-haired and entirely age-inappropriate fishing bride, was more than embarrassed by all this, and I could hardly blame her. Nineteen-year-old Helena, who was not only beautiful but smart, could have had her pick of Hutterite men. But now she was bound, in the accusing sight of Minnesota game and fish authorities anyway, to a 32-year-old "world man." As much as I wanted to, I never had the heart to tease her about this, and eventually everyone forgot about the whole sordid episode.

We loaded up on bait and a few odds and ends and bused our way down to the south fork of the Crow River, which flowed past a dam in the middle of Hutchinson's business district. The dam, which often was covered by a frozen cascade in winter, was surrounded by a small park near the main street and next to several stores and other businesses.

Though it looked nothing like the remote and overgrown fishing holes I had frequented along the Mississippi as a boy, the river was full of fish, especially the local favorite, Northern pike, and before long, I had caught my first-ever walleye.

Aside from being the place we usually went to when we went to "town," Hutchinson was something of a notable place in our part of Minnesota. With about 13,000 people, it was one of the larger towns due west of the Twin Cities and had a history dating back to before the Civil War.

A statue near downtown, overlooking the river, depicted Chief Little Crow, a Lakota Indian killed by a local farmer a year after the 1862 Sioux Uprising, during which Hutchinson was besieged for a time.

A sign near the city limits also reminded travelers that Hutchinson was the hometown of artist LeRoy Neiman, known for his rather splashy and impressionistic paintings of American sports figures. The Hutterites, of course, had no idea who LeRoy Neiman was, nor most of the people he painted, and so paid this little mind.

One thing I do remember striking their fancy was the fact that Hutchinson had the country's second-oldest municipal park system, trailing only New York City in making this innovation. Several times I had this pointed out to me by someone as something truly worth knowing. This sort of minutiae, and not the broader strokes of the culture around them, was of much greater interest to the Hutterian mind and, for awhile, to mine.

Our fishing trip stretched well into the evening, which had turned slightly cooler but no less oppressive. The barometer seemed to plummet at intervals, accompanied by vague reports of thunder someplace in the distance. By the time we returned home, around 8 p.m., the evening was still bright, but with thunderstorms clearly looming several counties away.

In our house, Sam cleaned and fried a few of the walleye we had reeled in, including my first catch, and we ate at our table until shortly after dark. Following this late supper, I walked over to the school to get our mail from the boxes at the bottom of the stairway. Out in the nearly pitch-black yard, I realized the wind had picked up considerably, and the heat had returned despite the hour. Under one of the streetlights near the school, a couple of boys were throwing horseshoes in the sandy pit someone had built near the school. Every few seconds, another toss would clang and echo out of the darkness.

As I walked back toward the house, with a floodlight near the playground vaguely illuminating the sidewalk, lightning flickered and then jolted several times to the west, and the clouds seemed to growl with still-distant thunder. The trees rattled around me as I stepped into our entryway and shut the door. At some point in the next hour, I went to bed and drifted into a quiet sleep.

The first thought I recall upon waking, suddenly and fully alert a few minutes before midnight, was that I must have forgotten to lock the outside door when I came in. Stepping into our hallway, I could literally see the wind rushing past, leaves and twigs born along on the whipping current. Pushing through to secure the door again, I finally noticed the familiar roar and whine of the tornado that was closing in on the colony from due south.

By this time, my wife had come out of the living room, where she had been reading, and I remember telling her to get Shelby and go into the hallway. In the living room, I strained to see out the front window, which was close to ground level and by now partially blocked by several downed tree limbs.

Throughout the storm, because the colony's emergency power generator had kicked into gear, all our lights remained on, a strange and disorienting counterpoint to the destruction and chaos wailing outside.

Though it was hard to see out, I recognized the telltale dust cloud on the ground to our east whenever the lightning flashed. "It's right on us," I shouted back to Duann, though she later said she never heard me.

Looking past the spinning debris to the north, I could see the 70-foot-high feed mill tower lit up by the next several lightning strikes, which hit every two or three seconds. By about the fourth or fifth strike, the tower was gone, along with the top of one of the large grain bins connected to it.

Others later said the wind had lasted for about two minutes, but from where I was watching and listening, it seemed to take 10 minutes or more to fully die away. The tornado, we would determine later, had not remained on the ground for any long stretches, but its whirling drafts had been enough to define a very clear path for nearly two miles.

Clearly, it was not a large or particularly destructive tornado, but it had passed so close by that its impact was brutal on our fragile metal buildings.

Outside, the wind fading, the streetlights had all shut down when their power lines were snarled by the wind and flying debris, so the darkness was complete except during lightning strikes. From our front window, with rain slashing by on the occasional gusts, I could see Jakob Decker running toward the shop, where he took care of the computer system.

Putting on my coat, I took a flashlight and decided to follow him. Fortunately, our door was not blocked and I could get outside without any difficulty. Having had a lot of experience with tornadoes as a storm spotter, I was careful to watch for the signs of any new spin-ups or for satellite twisters that could overtake us in seconds. Making my way slowly toward the shop, I trained the flashlight on the extensive debris and wreckage that covered the ground. I could see that the feed mill leg was definitely gone, but that it had fallen to the east instead of collapsing onto the mill itself.

I also could see that the houses, all of them with lights on because of the generator, had not been seriously damaged at all. Neither had the kitchen or school, which had only one broken window in an upstairs classroom. The shop, however, was another matter. As I made the corner behind the kitchen and walked past the trees of the second shelter belt, I could see the long narrow shop building no longer had half of its roof.

Considerable debris had been lifted from inside and spun all over the premises, including sheets of stainless steel which could have sliced a person in two if they had been struck by one out in the open. I also could see that the shop's concrete walls were still intact, as was the garage where all of the colony's vehicles and most of its trucks and farm equipment were parked.

The storm had wreaked the most havoc directly on the shop itself. Jakob had already entered the shop when I arrived, but I decided not to chance the darkness and the minefield of downed girders and ceiling rafters that I knew waited inside. Walking back toward the school, I met Conrad in his electrician's pickup and got in. I told him what I had seen at the shop, and together we drove toward the section road to see what lay beyond the colony.

Right away, we saw an electric transformer arcing next to the road into Paul Renner's farm on the other side of the section road due north of the colony. Paul's farm at some point had fallen into a state of functional disrepair. His large dairy barn, which he still used, had collapsed on one side, apparently in a snowstorm, and the rest of the yard was cluttered and a chaos of farm equipment.

Paul's wife, Gretel, who was an amiable neighbor, shared their small house with him, while Paul's elderly mother lived in a small trailer about 30 yards away. Though the colony had offered several times to help Paul clean up his place, he always declined and quickly withdrew back into his familiar world, a circle of commonplace things and animals that many remote Minnesota farmers knew very well.

As lightning continued to slash the sky to the northeast, Conrad got out and cleared the sparking, writhing power lines from Paul's road, which cut through a muddy field only recently seeded with corn. When Conrad opened his truck door, I noticed for the first time that the wind had shifted back to the south, carrying the sound of the tornado sirens all the way from Gibbon.

"If Paul still has a barn now, I won't believe it," Conrad said. I could see in the lightning that somehow Paul's collapsed milking parlor was exactly as it had been for the past several years, apparently none the worse, or mercifully improved, for the events of the past hour.

Conrad, pelted by a cold rain now, jumped back in the truck and drove past the colony feed mill, which is when we saw the real extent of the damage to the shop and to the mill, which had lost some of its siding but was still standing. In the mill office, Arnie Kleinsasser was looking at the online satellite farm reports, confirming that Sibley, McLeod, and Renville counties, our immediate locus, were under a continuing tornado warning.

Outside, the air still crackled with rain and menace. Looking at the radar, however, I could see the worst was past and that the skies were clearing all the way west into South Dakota. Just then, Joel drove up in another pickup, and he and I went across the county road and followed the storm debris to one of our neighbors about two miles away.

We found him in his yard, his lights also mysteriously still on, examining his foundation in the intermittent dark. It was clear that the house had shifted several feet and turned on its base, a sign of the twisting lift that tornadoes unleash on such structures, even just in passing.

Back at the colony, I walked into the entryway of the white house where about a dozen women and girls were milling about in their bathrobes and hastily-donned skirts, or *kitteln*. One of the wives, still clearly rattled from being awakened by the storm, asked what I had seen.

"Was it a tornado, Robert? What was it?"

I told them I thought it had been a small tornado, but that it had not been on the ground for very long and that none of the houses were damaged. I said the shop and feedmill were in bad shape, especially the shop. I tried to assure them there were no more storms on the way, at least not for a few hours, and that it seemed no one had been hurt.

"What happened to the shop, Robert?" one of the women asked.

"It doesn't have a roof anymore," I said. "I'd imagine the wind caught up one of the overhead doors and caved it in, which made the air rush out through the ceiling and took the roof with it. There's steel every place, too. I saw Jakob go in to check the computers, but I wouldn't go in there and I hope no one else does. It's a good way to get hurt or worse if it caves in any, or if the walls should go."

As the women drifted off to their apartments, I walked back to our house and lay down on the couch, still wearing my coat in the wet, chilly air. Duann and Shelby had already gone back to bed.

The next morning most of us woke early to an overcast sky. For a moment, still half-asleep, I forgot what had happened the night before, so was startled when I looked out our living room window into the chaotic yard. As my memories of the night came rushing back, Sam appeared at our door, already getting dressed for church and rubbing his eyes.

"That's quite a scene," I told Sam, his white Sunday suspenders down around his waist.

"What do you mean?"

"I mean what happened last night, the tornado."

Sam looked confused for a moment.

"The what?"

"The tornado. We got hit by a tornado last night."

Somehow, Sam and Greta both had slept through the entire thing, apparently not hearing the roaring wind or all the other disruption outside. Like ours, their house was partially underground, but on the side opposite the tornado's path, so the noise must not have been as invasive. In all the uproar, I had not thought to check on them or make sure they knew what was going on. Sam stepped to our window and pressed his nose to the glass.

"I should go down," he said, pulling up his suspenders and reaching for his black coat in the entryway.

"The shop is kaput, Sam. It got the worst of it. The roof is all inside and there's steel all over the place."

"Did you see it? What about the machines? Can we get to the brake or the shear?"

"I didn't go in, but Jakob did. I don't know what it's like in there."

I followed him out into the yard as we started toward the shop. I soon saw the yard was full of people, milling aimlessly and staring silently, like people always do after a shock or disaster of any scale. The sight of men and women, young and old, as well as every child on the place, wandering about in their Sunday best amid the storm's furious rubble was strange and incongruous.

Where the day before we had a neat and tidy colony, a tad on the cluttered side by Hutterite standards, but well-kept and doted on nonetheless, disorder had raised the roof. The treetops were flung with debris, perhaps even from neighboring farms, and all manner of trash and scrap littered the ground.

The yard near the houses was bad enough, but rounding the corner behind the kitchen, the worst damage of all came into view. The shop, center of our collective commerce and livelihood, and the primary source of our income, looked like a bomb had gone off inside.

The metal roof was sundered and even obliterated in some places, and what appeared to be large, man-sized paper wads — actually metal roof and siding material cast skyward and crushed by the storm — were strewn along a clear diagonal for more than a mile to the northeast. That would be the tornado's most obvious calling card, at least in my memory.

In the shop, some of the men were already trying to get through the collapsed aftermath to some of the equipment. None of the machinery appeared to have been badly damaged, but everything was buried under several layers of wood, steel, and the shredded paper and cellulose insulation the walls and ceilings had been tightly filled with. This insulation, which in its normal state resembled gray oatmeal flakes or dirty snow, now looked like dried dollops of cement and adhered, soaked by the rain, to every visible surface in the shop.

In some places it stood a foot or more deep. Sam knew immediately the hydraulics of the big machinery would be full of this insulation, and he passed the word not to turn anything on until it had been examined and repaired. Clarence Wollman and a couple of young men were working with chainsaws, trying to cut their way into where one of the forklifts was parked.

"Sam, we've got to get the forklifts out first," Clarence called out. "Then we can use those to pull everything else out with."

This seemed like the only workable plan given the scale and severity of the damage, and soon all three forklifts were parked in the yard, spackled like everything else in the shop with a layer of dried insulation.

The word already had gone around that *Lehr* was canceled that morning, and so most of the people returned to their homes for a slow, rather grief-stricken breakfast before the recovery work began in earnest. I had thought that if the community needed to come together, physically and spiritually, as we were supposed to during a church service, this would have been the time to do it.

Hutterite practicality ruled, however, and it was decided that work on reopening the shop would begin immediately. Besides, I had seen David Vetter in the yard, and he seemed as dazed and upset, perhaps even more, as everyone else. I tried to imagine his viewpoint, as the temporal and spiritual leader of a community he had helped build from the ground up, despite all the usual personal and financial obstacles that all colonies, or secular businesses, faced.

A child of the Depression, he seemed deeply aware of how fragile an agricultural economy could be, and though Starland was extremely prosperous, he always appeared to be more than a little uncomfortable with our wealth, or at least with how it influenced our lifestyle.

Still, I felt conflicted that at such a time of great need, we could not see the use of coming together in prayer, or at least collective humility, to find our way through this. As usual, my understanding of communal spirituality was still vague and unformed and, as it always would be, very different from the typical Hutterite expression. There also were other issues at work in this decision that I was not aware of yet – personal and spiritual divisions within the community that the storm magnified even more. Many of these were merely interpersonal spats, the kinds of disagreements that arise whenever people live among one another in close quarters. Others had to do with discord over the general direction the community was following, from its involvement in prosperous commerce to its relationship, or lack of it, with the Bruderhof Communities. The spiritual disagreements were harder to define, but had a lot to do with a desire among some to adhere to strict traditions, while others wanted the colonies to return to the early Hutterian zeal for mission work and winning converts. The storm, just as it had torn the roof from our shop, also aggravated these brooding disputes by bringing a certain chaos to the daily proceedings in the community. With our familiarity and comfort in disrepair, it was easy for conflict to explode.

As it turned out, we would not have church as a community for several weeks, after most of the cleanup was done and the shop was running almost at the same speed as before. When I didn't find this spiritual alienation puzzling, I found it deeply disappointing and disorienting.

That morning, as I stood next to the carwash, full of insulation and with half a roof above it, people milling about me in shades of shock and outright fear, Josh Vetter emerged from the mob and looked me straight in the eye.

"Well, Robert Vetter. What say you to this? Are we going to give up now, or do we say what Job said?"

Josh Vetter, because of his age and bearing, seemed to be one of the most traditional Hutterites I had met so far. I would learn later, though, that his strict and sometimes heavy-bearing character belied a subtle understanding of what would bring a family like ours to the community. Before long, Josh would become something of a role model for me and a true friend.

Before I could attempt to answer, Tim Decker, the farm boss and work distributor, walked up as well.

"Look at it," he said, his usually dark expression even more bereft this morning. "Look at our proud shop. God is saying something very serious to us here. Don't you think so, Robert?"

"Maybe you're right," I said.

"I just hope we listen."

I looked at Josh Vetter as Tim headed toward one of his tractors.

I asked, "What did Job say, Josh Vetter?"

"He said, 'The Lord giveth and the Lord taketh away.' But will we be able to say what he said next?"

"What was that, Josh Vetter?"

"What, you don't know? Boy, you Catholics really don't know your Bible."

"I guess," I said. "But what did he say next?"

Josh's voice, sometimes sharp and stentorian, though usually with the hint of a smile somewhere in evidence, grew quiet and perhaps even slightly doubtful, as if he couldn't quite grasp Job and the tornado and all the rest of this himself.

"What did he say next? Next he said, 'Thanks be to God.'"

Josh was right, of course, but after a shock like this, I didn't imagine even the most pious Hutterite thanking God or anyone else after such a blow, at least not yet. Because we had not lived in the colony for very long, we didn't feel such a personal loss after the storm. We had not grown so deeply attached and invested in the place as our neighbors had. After all, it had been their years of labor and faith and struggle that had built this place, only to see half of it dashed to pieces in a few minutes of belligerent wind.

That afternoon the worst would begin to lift, though, as work crews from other colonies, mostly from South Dakota, started arriving to lend a hand in the cleanup work. As that first grim day wore on, progress began to be seen in small, then much more pronounced ways.

After a long and ponderous dinner in the kitchen — an attempt at restoring normalcy that all of us appreciated, I think — Joel walked about the colony with a video camera, documenting the damage and offering a running commentary on what had happened and who had come to help bail us out.

In places, he tried to make light of what was in front of us all, hoping perhaps to ameliorate some of the gloom and doubt a lot of people were experiencing. Much of the video was silent, though, other than the gentle prairie wind buffeting the microphone and the raucous buzz of chainsaws as the work crews dismantled the collapsed shop roof and revealed the extent of the damage within. Even the usually talkative Joel found himself short of words as he recorded the cleanup.

"What ... a ... mess," he said again and again, until it became sort of a running joke around the colonies once the video had made the rounds. People would repeat "what ... a ... mess" in its many vocal permutations, and then laugh in that casual way that Hutterites have of laughing at their own misfortune.

A few weeks later, at Crystal Spring Colony in Manitoba, someone would come up and ask if I had seen the video, which had come back with a work crew sent down to Starland to help. I said I hadn't.

"You should watch it sometime," I was told. "All you see is pile after pile and then you get Joel's voice, over and over, saying, 'What ... a ... mess.' It's better than Laurel and Hardy. Do you know them, Robert Vetter?"

Though our shop was rendered inoperative by the storm, we were at least partially back in business on Tuesday morning, and for a short time, my welding table and the parts I made for the colony in Canada were our sole source of income. On Monday, once the majority of the roof wreckage had been pulled out of the shop, my welding tools were moved out and reassembled in the parking garage.

Though it was dark and stuffy back there — we had to keep the doors and windows closed or my welding gases would blow away — and there was no ventilation to speak of, it was decided that I would go back to work right away. It wasn't much — we made about a dollar for each part I welded — but it was something, and officially anyway, it would mean we were back in operation less than 48 hours after the storm. I was willing to do whatever I could and immediately set about welding, earning money for the colony, while everyone else worked at the cleanup and repairs.

I admit that I enjoyed the irony more than a little. Here, after all, was the worldly *mensch*, the wanderer from the corrupt and ugly morass of American society, the interloper from a strange and faraway place, providing — temporarily anyway — the colony's main source of financial support.

The astonishing thing was that the people around me seemed to see the irony as well and were genuinely grateful for my few meager efforts. It was something in any event, and given the circumstances, it was enough to gain me a peculiar sense of status in the community that I had not enjoyed before.

In the weeks that followed, the shop slowly got back into business, and a new roof was constructed above the work floor, as well as a new elevator tower for the feed mill. Just before our family left for a period of work in Canada, I ran a nail through my right foot, becoming the first person actually injured, however slightly, in the aftermath of the storm.

While we were away in Manitoba, however, the steward, David Jr., fell from a wall in the shop while helping with repairs, tumbling nearly 20 feet onto a concrete floor and fracturing an elbow and his pelvis. Other than Junior, no one was seriously hurt during events related to the storm.

Though Starland was never hit by a tornado again during our time there, the community did have a few close calls. The most treacherous came while our family was away on another trip to Manitoba, where I was working with several others on the English translation of the *Kleine-Geschichtsbuch* at Crystal Spring, which was about 25 miles south of Winnipeg.

On Sunday, March 29, 1998, we were visiting a sister colony in Manitoba's Interlake region, so we didn't hear the news of the cluster of tornadoes that devastated two towns south of Starland until nearly midnight, when we drove back to Crystal Spring and heard a radio report on the CBC as we passed through Winnipeg.

The next day, on calling home, we learned that the storm system that produced the tornadoes had been headed directly toward Sibley County before it broke east and moved toward the small college town of St. Peter, a few miles north of Mankato. After nearly leveling the town of Comfrey, southwest of Starland, the storm continued on a path that would have brought it directly across our land.

Instead, the early-season storm, which hit at a time when snow remained on the ground in other years, seemed to follow the course of the Minnesota River. It just missed New Ulm and the small towns of Courtland and Nicollet before dropping a large, violent F3 tornado that would roll down onto St. Peter shortly before 5:30 p.m.

The home of Gustavus Adolphus College, which overlooks the town from a steep bluff, St. Peter was home to about 10,000 people when the storm struck. The tornado made a direct hit on the hilltop campus, damaging every building and destroying more than 1,000 trees before slamming into the rest of the town, which was notable for its quaint and well-commerced business district and neighborhoods of Victorian and Craftsman-style houses, many of which were totally destroyed.

While St. Peter before the storm had been a town full of trees and attractive sidestreets, afterward it was virtually denuded. Because it hit at a time when most people were at home, or at least off the streets, only one death resulted from the St. Peter tornado. A six-year-old boy riding in a car with his mother was killed when the tornado overtook them just west of town.

I often thought that if the 1996 tornado had hit Starland during the day instead of at midnight, or when people were out in the yard some afternoon or working in the shop, the losses would have been exponentially worse. It was bad enough as it was, but when I consider how much more severe it could have been, or the possibility there was for grave injury or fatalities, the potential for devastation is indescribable.

chapter
SIXTEEN

The late winter of 1996-1997 was another of crystalline cold and obliterating snowstorms, like most winters in Minnesota. This winter, though, our family was awaiting the arrival of our second child. When Lydia was born on April 1, 1997, it was the first time an outsider's child had been born among the colonies in many years. Of course, in a Hutterite community, the birth of a child is cause for great joy, and Lydia's arrival was no different.

That winter a celestial visitor also arrived in the sky above the frozen prairie. On March 22, the Hale-Bopp comet, later deemed a "great" comet for the lustrous illumination it imparted on many nights, made its perigee, or closest pass to the Earth. That night we took an old telescope from the supply closet in the school and set it out in a clear area near the playground, where members of the community could stop and observe the comet as it passed us by.

For the Hutterites, as for many other cultures, comets have long been seen as grim portents, or at least as possible messengers from God. The *Great Chronicle*, written in an age when such phenomena were barely understood even by the intellectual elite, makes mention of several medieval comets, the movements and durations of which are carefully noted.

A comet that passed in 1577 seemed of special interest not only to the author of the Hutterite history book, but to artists and astronomers of the age. This "Great Comet of 1577" was noted in the *Great Chronicle*'s surviving handwritten codices with a drawing of a star trailing a brushy dust plume. This "remarkably bright comet," according to the *Chronicle*, was "first observed in the evening of November 13, the Wednesday after Martinmas."

The night before, this same comet was observed in full bloom by the famed Danish astronomer Tycho Brahe, who recorded it with a drawing in his notebook and used his calculations to determine that the tails of comets, which he described as celestial objects and not optical illusions as Galileo thought, actually point away from the sun. The comet was noted in much of Europe's literature of the time, and a contemporary engraving shows the large, dazzling comet spanning the sky above Prague. This astonishing sight came amid an era, from 1565 to 1591, of relative peace for the Hutterites known as their "Golden Years." If this visitor in the night sky raised any concerns among the Hutterites, they were not recorded in the history book.

Other comets, however, were noted in hindsight for the grim events they seemed to precede, such as the flight and persecutions that befell the communities during the Thirty Years War. In an entry from the *Great Chronicle* dated 1618 appears this note about such a comet:

"On November 29 ... around four o'clock in the morning, an extraordinary comet appeared. It was brilliant and had a very long tail such as is rarely seen. After that, it appeared each morning a little earlier until it rose exactly at midnight. The time when it rose changed gradually from morning to midnight and from midnight to evening. This covered a period of four weeks, namely from November 29 until the end of December. It was watched with great awe and terror and was last seen close to the North Star, where it faded away. In the years following, we were to learn, with much suffering and sorrow, what it had signified."

This comet of 1618, which was seen across Europe and the Near East, is thought by some astronomers to have been a cluster of as many as three different comets. Its impressive appearance is recorded in other sources from the same era, as are other comets that appeared during the war's brutal duration — as many as 18, according to some sources — in which the Hutterites faced bitter tribulations in their Moravian homeland. From this point on, if notations in the *Great Chronicle* are any indication, the Hutterites watched subsequent comets with special care, such as one that appeared in December 1652. "God alone will reveal its meaning," the often foreboding chronicler wrote.

Likewise for another comet that shone on Christmas Eve 1664, "its significance ... known to God alone." This comet, or another like it, appeared again the following January 4, followed by another sighting on April 5, all carefully noted in the history book, all among a time of considerable difficulty for the struggling, harassed communities.

If someone had been writing down Hutterian history in 1997, they could not have neglected to mention Hale-Bopp, which was one of the most vivid and enduring comets of the 20th century. In the colony its nightly appearances were cause for curiosity, if not outward alarm.

In our experience with the tornado less than a year before, several people in the community glimpsed divine disfavor.

Others elsewhere were more concerned, and even grew deranged, by the comet's significance. The same night the comet was closest to Earth, a monastic-styled religious cult in California, Heaven's Gate, committed mass suicide, believing Hale-Bopp to be trailed by extraterrestrials who were going to "recycle" or cleanse the planet of all impurities.

Several days later, when this suicide was discovered, it reminded me of the doomsayers who said that in 1973, comet Kohoutek — perhaps the last century's most heralded celestial fizzle — would destroy all life on the planet when its tail whisked our atmosphere on Christmas Day. If this was not grim enough, another group, the Children of God, said Kohoutek foretold a global catastrophe that would occur in January 1974, plus or minus 40 days.

Hale-Bopp apparently bore us no ill will. On Tuesday, April 1, the same day the comet achieved perihelion, or its closest pass to the Sun, our daughter Lydia was born in the Hutchinson hospital. That night would have been among the comet's brightest appearances if we had not been in the midst of a late-season blizzard, which was followed by yet another the following Sunday while we were all in church.

The first blizzard had followed several days of rain and flash flooding up in McLeod County, giving us a challenging trip to the hospital when it came time for Lydia to be born.

Where snow did not cover the road, frozen floodwater, often in the form of black ice, did. The blizzard, which blew up across a prairie already cleared of previous snows, dredged up great quantities of black earth with its winds and spackled everything in its way with thick, wet snow and dark mud.

Lydia came to us after several months of fear and struggle for Duann. Because of several bouts of premature labor, Duann had remained on constant bed rest for nearly two months before our second daughter's arrival. This experience would repeat itself before our son, Aidan, was born in August 1999.

Following Lydia's birth — she and Duann came home from the hospital between blizzards — Duann entered what the Hutterites term a mother's "weeks," when the woman remains at home with her child for about 40 days, relieved of all work responsibilities and receiving special food meant to help restore her strength and fortify the baby's milk.

Unfortunately, because she had remained at home for nearly two months before Lydia was born, Duann was feeling a bit isolated and house-trapped by the time her "weeks" began in earnest. Because we were not colony natives, we also were at something of a disadvantage during this time.

Traditionally, a woman's mother comes, usually from the woman's home colony, to help her daughter care for her new baby during part of this lying-in time. We, of course, had no colony relatives, and it was not convenient for Duann's mother, Martha, to travel to Minnesota from Arkansas because of illness in the family. Though Duann's parents visited the colony a few times, her father's slow battle with cancer kept them closer to home most of the time.

Instead, Katherine Wollman, Herman's wife, stood in as Duann's "mother," followed later by Angela Decker, our teenage babysitter, and some of the other colony girls who went and fetched things and took care of household chores such as laundry and cleaning while Duann rested with Lydia.

After a prescribed time, it was traditional for the recovering mother to make an appearance at *Lehr*, which Duann did after three or four weeks. Meanwhile, our family got to eat our meals at home and enjoy some of the special foods — such as noodle soup, chicken broth, waffles, and an enriched and very sweet form of toasted *zweibach* — typically set aside for the new mothers by the *kranken kuch*, or "sick cook," who looked after such cases.

Lydia's arrival seemed to cement our place in the community a bit more and helped Duann forge a new link with the other young mothers there. We had decided on Lydia's name in part because it was a traditional *Hutterisch* name we liked and also because our colony did not have anyone else called that.

However, we did know four Lydias at other colonies in the States and Canada, and these women all sent our new daughter a "name dress" not long after she was born. Name dresses are sent to a little girl by women who share her first name. All of these Lydias, including the minister's wife from Neuhof, sent a dress that a toddler would wear, so our daughter got to grow into her special clothes.

Other women, from Starland and elsewhere, sent Lydia some small bonnets, called *muetzen*. Christy Wipf, our next-door neighbor, knitted her some tiny wool slippers, while other women in the colony donated cloth diapers, all homemade, and other baby clothes.

SEVENTEEN

I have been asked many times whether we kept in touch with the outside world while we were living in the colony. This depended on what we were staying in touch with. Because we read newspapers and listened to news on the radio, the lack of televisions really did not have an isolating effect, other than that none of us had seen certain shows that held the rest of the country rapt for years at a time. When we finally acceded to the advent of the Internet, starting in our shop and soon after in the school, the world drew even closer, and our awareness of it gained a certain currency it had not had before.

The day of the terrorist attacks of September 11, 2001, was a singular occasion for the colony, a time when we seemed as much in touch with the rest of the world as anyone else.

As it was that day in New York City, I remember that Tuesday morning was bright and cool in central Minnesota. As I often did, I walked over to the shop shortly after breakfast ended at 7:30 and, after opening up my office, began scanning the news online, which I did most mornings.

I always read the same dozen or so news sites every day, starting with *The New York Times*, CNN and the British newspaper *The Guardian*, and then looking at various other news sites before we really started doing any meaningful work for the day. That morning, I was probably the first person in the colony to become aware that anything was wrong in New York, when the CNN site posted its first bulletins about part of the World Trade Center being on fire, apparently after what was described as a small private plane had struck one of the towers.

I immediately thought of an incident in July 1945 when a World War II-era B-25 bomber had gone off course in fog and struck the Empire State Building. Early photos from the Trade Center that morning, however, showed a crystalline sky sullied only by the gusts of black smoke pouring from the north tower.

Meanwhile, in their houses, several families had started listening, as was their habit, to the morning news on National Public Radio, which also broke in with news of the first impact. Before long, *The New York Times'* Web site was reporting the second plane hitting the building. Because I had been reading only sketchy reports with no narration and few photos, the significance of this second impact escaped me for the moment.

I actually thought, as I looked at my computer screen, that something must have gone terribly wrong in some air-traffic control tower somewhere, leaving jets to swarm into the hazardous caverns of lower Manhattan. Just then, Brandon Wollman appeared at our door and said he had heard this was some sort of terrorist attack. Not long after, the *Times* Web site went down, and CNN's became jammed briefly.

I switched to the *Guardian*, which had a bureau near the Trade Center and had a very informative story unfolding on its Web site. This was about the time of the attack on the Pentagon, which was first reported as an assault with shoulder-fired rockets launched from near the facility's helipad.

Shortly after this, erroneous reports about a bombing at the State Department also were posted, along with photos of workers fleeing the White House and other landmarks. Something that minutes before had seemed so strangely innocuous to us out on the prairie – an unfortunate plane striking a monolithic tower few of us had ever seen in person – had become a matter of astronomical violence and, it would ensue, international tragedy in a very short time.

At some point I realized the shop was still entirely empty, and Brandon and I wandered over to the school where a television antenna had been rigged up on the roof and the colony's only set rolled into what used to be our church room downstairs. When I walked in, virtually the entire community was gathered there, silently watching CBS, the only network available to us without cable, as it switched between New York and Washington and began reporting about another plane someplace, believed to have been hijacked like the others and pointed toward Washington.

As the images of the two burning towers filled the quavering TV screen, I realized that my wife and all of our children had entered the room, watching this along with the rest of the world. I got up and took our two daughters outside to play when CBS began showing the desperate jumpers plunging from the blazing towers.

After I returned, my mind immediately went back to when I had lived in New York during summer school, and the day when I had traveled by elevator to the top of the north tower, mostly on a lark, but also to see if I could find a person I had met who worked somewhere up there.

In those days, almost a decade before the 1993 bombing of the Trade Center, security had been virtually nonexistent, at least on the floors I had been on. Entering at the ground lobby, I had stumbled onto an express elevator, where a custodian asked if I wanted to "go high," to the tower's upper reaches. After a moment of consideration, I said, "Why not?" and we started our journey into the sky, getting off at a mid-level lobby, and then jetting the rest of the way, along with a few stragglers that late summer morning, as far as it seemed I could go.

Looking out from a window near the elevator landing, a good 90 floors up, the sky that day was clear and open, just as it appeared on the television screen that bizarre September morning.

I returned to my seat near the front of the room just as CBS reported the collapse, then thought to be partial, of the south tower. As the initial plume of dust and debris began to spread out, the total absence of the tower, and the empty quadrant of sky where it had been only seconds before, struck me very deeply.

Looking around me, I realized I was on my feet, and that almost everyone else in the room also was standing, stunned, totally silent in the face of this. It was not long before the second tower also fell, this time in clear view of the television cameras, and I saw in those few seconds, as we watched the tower pancake floor by floor with increasing velocity, that this was something apocalyptic, a calamity that would have consequences for a long time to come.

The people around me seemed to have no vocabulary to express what any of this meant to them. Some, I imagined, especially the more vengeance-minded who saw God as a great retributionist, probably were counting up the souls they believed were streaming into perdition even as we watched, having failed to embrace the same religion as a bunch of Russian-peasant communalists far away on the prairie. Others, I thought, might have had the opposite, more merciful view, while most, including me, had no idea what to make of any of this. Almost immediately, I just wanted to flee, to put this behind me somehow, to start forgetting by simply not looking anymore.

From somewhere far back in the room, I heard a woman's voice that I did not recognize at first, but later realized belonged to one of the older people in the community, someone who had experienced great need and want as a child in the Depression, and who had lived a life much harder than most others in the colony. I don't remember if she spoke in *Hutterisch* or English, which were nearly interchangeable for me now, but the meaning was clear right away.

"So this is how it's all going to end," she said. "So this is how it's all going to end."

I left the room and went to our house, taking my children along with me from the playground where they had wandered. In our living room, I closed the door, drew the curtains and lay down on the sofa. In a few moments, I got up and turned the radio to NPR and the continuing news of the attacks.

I lay down again as the radio droned. It, and the television in the school, would remain on, nearly 24 hours a day, for a week or more. After a few days, I realized I was waiting, like a lot of people all over the world, for someone to explain exactly what had happened, and why.

These answers were impossible, of course, and were left for all of us to decipher alone, however we could.

Knowing that we were going to be leaving the colony in a few months, I wondered about the world I was going back to, and whether it was any different from the one I occupied from within the colony's cool protections.

I also felt, for the first time in nearly six years, the surge of adrenaline that reporters get when faced with a big story. It had begun as I watched the south tower collapse, and I had nearly not recognized it.

If tragedies like this were going to hit us, then I wanted to cope as I had with other terrible events — by being in their midst and writing about them. It was a sense I thought I had thoroughly repressed or allowed to go delinquent in myself over the past six years. But as I stared at the curtains in our house that morning, I realized it had come back.

That night the sky, which often was filled with blinking lights and faint contrails reflected by the moon, was strangely still, with all but emergency air flights still grounded across the country. As I walked toward the shop, the moon itself became visible from behind some apple trees, a crescent waning into its last quarter. A nearby planet mimicked with immediate irony the symbol of Islam.

The next day I had a medical appointment in Minneapolis. As I did whenever these appointments came up, I walked to the garage for a car and left early in the morning while it was still dark. As I often did on these trips, I took some back roads from the colony out to the main highway.

As I wound across the curves and right angles of farmland, the corn still tall and sturdy a month before harvest, the news of the day before was inescapable. Every radio station had gone to all-talk formats, it seemed, with any number of opinions and speculations about the attacks being aired, including comments on the appearance of the moon the night before, which would become a topic for conspiracy theorists and Muslim-bashers alike.

I reached Minneapolis just as the sun rose. The sight of the skyscrapers downtown, some of which had been evacuated as a precaution less than 24 hours before, were a visual reminder of what had happened. At St. Mary's Hospital, near the University of Minnesota campus overlooking the Mississippi River, I had a clear view of downtown and of the interstate, where it seemed a much-enhanced police presence was out in force. In the hospital lobby a long line of people waited to donate blood.

On the 12th floor where my doctor's office was located, the mood seemed grim and reticent. When I went in to see Dr. Patrick O'Laughlin, with whom I had developed a fairly close relationship, I was not surprised when the first thing he asked me was, "Did you see the moon last night?"

A few blocks away near the corner of Cedar and Riverside, a large and robust neighborhood made up mostly of Somali immigrants, the street was quiet. Shortly after noon on any other day, the sidewalks would have been filled with worshippers emerging from midday prayers at a mosque in a nearby high-rise apartment building. This day, however, the people seemed very reserved and frightened as they peered out from shops and restaurants. As one of the few white interlopers in evidence in this part of town, I sensed they were looking at me.

Given the news of retribution against Muslims around the country since the day before, I realized they had good reason to be cautious. I felt quite acutely the fear in their dark faces, men and women alike, nearly all immigrants, even as I willed myself to detach and stand merely as an objective observer of their circumstances. But detachment, I had learned as a journalist, was not always preferable, much less convenient. Sometimes, it was better to feel, especially if it helped convey the angst and uncertainty of a particular moment or place.

In the colony I had become accustomed to feeling a range of unfamiliar emotions in certain situations, so it was hard to stop, even to insulate myself against a form of apprehension as palpable as what these people seemed to experience. I wondered if this was how blacks in the South had felt, even during my own childhood, whenever racial violence threatened to brim over.

In the South I was not attuned to the feelings of "otherness" such as these Somali people lived with now. In the South racism was a paradox none of us had the answer to. Here it seemed much more predatory, as if violence could spin up from the most innocuous places — among a group of people milling about after a prayer service, or out of a clear blue sky before the calming advent of autumn.

Back at the colony that evening people were still gathered in the reassuring glow of the television in the school, still watching CBS and what apparently was nonstop news coverage of the attacks and the frantic search through the Trade Center wreckage in New York. It still seemed conceivable that someone could have survived and been awaiting rescue, though it also seemed very doubtful, given the magnitude of the calamity and the sheer weight and immensity of the fallen towers.

Later, on nightwatch, I sat in the room alone and switched the set back on. I watched for about an hour, and then turned it off again. Nothing had changed, nor would it.

A few minutes after I left, another man, unable to sleep, walked in, his suspenders down around his hips, and turned the television back on — a scene of restless confusion that played out all over the country on this night.

~

Even if we were totally aware of what was happening during the 9/11 attacks, and even witnessed some of the calamity live on television, people in most other Hutterite colonies did not. The weekend before the attacks, a plain Mennonite historian from Pennsylvania, Amos Hoover, along with fellow Mennonite historians James Lowry and Gary Waltner, had stopped in at Starland to spend a few days. Ostensibly, they came to visit me, because I'd met Amos and James in Pennsylvania back in 1999 when I spoke at Elizabethtown College.

But Amos, who has a large collection of old Anabaptist books, including a sterling archive of old copies of the *Martyrs Mirror* and the *Ausbund*, the Amish hymnal, really wanted to head west to Bonhomme Colony in South Dakota, where he knew he finally could get a look at the surviving handwritten *Chronicle* in Jakob Waldner's humid parlor.

After spending the weekend at Starland, the group left sometime Monday afternoon and drove the several hours to Bonhomme, where they spent all of Tuesday, September 11, with access to no media whatsoever. The next day the group left Bonhomme and drove north to Watertown, South Dakota, where they checked into a motel. It was only then, when they saw a newspaper and turned on a television, that they realized what had happened the day before.

"It was like we had spent a couple of days on the moon," Amos said of the media blackout at Bonhomme. "We came out of there and headed for Watertown and all of a sudden it was like the world was ending. I actually thought for a minute that it was."

chapter
EIGHTEEN

We had known we would leave Starland for several months, actually more than half a year, before we physically moved ourselves to south-central Kansas, where I was due to start a job as assistant editor of *Mennonite Weekly Review*. The job was offered to me in May 2001, and would begin the following January.

Those intervening months were a time of great trial and even torment for us, as well as of anticipation. In many ways, because we knew we were soon to forsake a life we thought we would always live, Duann and I became deeply disillusioned not only about the colony and what went on there, but about all life in the outside world.

It was easy enough to become disillusioned about the colony. Around the time we decided to leave, the entire community had endured more than five years of intense turmoil, from within and without. As outsiders who had no way to cope with any of this upheaval, or no families with whom to bond or weather such storms, we had become not only spiritually but physically and mentally exhausted.

By far, the most tiresome aspect of life for us was the constant harping and questioning by many in the community about the Hutterites' link with the Bruderhof Communities. With several families having left for the Bruderhof over the years, only to return in some cases and ultimately leave again, we felt caught in the crossfire of not only familial strife but a very fundamental religious conflict.

In the Bruderhof, a certain authoritarianism seemed to prevail. There also was a keen idealism in the Bruderhof that sanctioned a good deal of public political activism and visible resistance on social issues such as the death penalty, war, and abortion. Though the Hutterites would have agreed with their former co-religionists on most of these matters, at least in principle, their approach was much more reticent and hands-off. Hutterites would never march in anti-war demonstrations, even though their own people had been martyred because of war countless times, nor would they consider overtures of sympathetic solidarity with groups such as the Catholic Church, as the Bruderhof sought to do.

Life among the Hutterites also was not guided as much by authority figures or strict rules but by a much more spontaneous kind of consensus. Though we followed a general schedule every day, and followed a set of traditions and basic practices and dressed a certain way, there was nothing regimented about our life in the colony, something the Bruderhof, with its much larger communities, could not adapt to. Though these differences might seem small at first glance, they evoked deep and often harsh dissent, and this was where we found our greatest frustration.

Our decision to leave, however, had less to do with these conflicts than it did with concerns for our children and their future. Because we have two daughters, both of us were concerned that their futures not be unfairly determined by the limits of the Hutterian lifestyle, which in the case of women could be perceived as quite repressive.

Though there are many strong, assertive and intelligent Hutterite women who live productive and even innovative lives in their colonies – especially in the area of education and business we felt that our daughters should grow up with a wider variety of choices about education, livelihood, and, if they choose, marriage and raising a family. In the end, we did not feel it was fair for our decision to live in the colony to predetermine most of the parameters of our children's lives. This predicament, along with the various conflicts that had been going on practically since we had arrived in the community, ultimately determined our decision to leave.

Though we felt we had valid reasons for leaving the colony, it still was not easy. First, we did not want to appear to leave in anger or create a fresh wave of strife when we announced our decision to depart. So many who had left before – both ethnic Hutterites and outsiders – had left quite a bit of scorched earth in their paths, doing a great deal of harm, we felt, to the people who chose to stay.

We did not harbor any ill will toward the community as a whole, or against any individuals, and we did not want to give anyone the impression that we did. As a result, we kept our decision to ourselves until less than a week before we actually moved away. This, of course, came as something of a shock to the people we loved and knew so well in the community.

However, it did not draw things out or allow conflicts to flare or intervene around what we were doing. Looking back, it seems that our approach to leaving surprised quite a few people who were used to others departing under stressful circumstances. In any event, we saw no purpose in trying to hurt anyone by leaving. If anything, we wanted people to know we still cared for them and wished that things could have been different.

Even though we kept our decision to ourselves for so long, this did not make matters any easier for Duann and me. For my part, knowing that we were going to leave raised an infinity of doubts about what we were doing. Some days it seemed I had changed my mind about leaving dozens of times.

In other ways, we still seemed very much a part of the community life. In June, I gave three presentations at Elizabethtown College in Pennsylvania during a conference on the media and its interaction with plain groups. Following this, I spent three weeks at the college's Young Center for Anabaptist and Pietist Studies, where I was made an honorary fellow, given an office and a place to stay on campus and the opportunity to write. I continued writing my columns for *Mennonite Weekly Review* and essays for various magazines and assisted in a class on communal societies being taught at Penn State.

In many ways I felt deeply fulfilled by being asked, and then being allowed by the community, to do this kind of work. At the same time, I felt that becoming sort of an "academic Hutterite" contradicted what we were really about. I felt that instead of remaining the anonymous, unknown person alone on the prairie, I was becoming a personage of some kind, giving earnest talks and lectures about the joys and vicissitudes of "communal life" and "radical Christianity."

Though the audiences I spoke to seemed sincere and interested, I began to feel like I was peddling a bill of goods — describing a culture that for the most part was not welcoming to outside people or influences, extolling a society of faith where my family was enduring entirely because of our own resolve. We had realized, after six years, that the issues that frustrated us would never change and might even get worse. We could choose to live with them and suffer the consequences, or we could move on, even if doing so was extremely painful.

About half the time I was away from the community that summer, I felt I was being a total hypocrite, a pretender to what once had been a radical observation of Christianity. The rest of the time, I felt a kind of renewal flowing through me, as if this time would help me return to the colony with refreshed ideals and a more vigorous tenacity to follow through with what I still considered to be a serious, vow-centered commitment.

I nearly had dropped out of the conference and the other activities I had planned for that summer, but felt obligated to attend because I had made those commitments well before we had decided for certain to leave. In all honesty, I also did not want to give up the chance to write for three weeks unhindered, or to be able to ponder, in relative peace and quiet, what lay ahead for our family. But then I realized: What about my wife and children? How did my going off on an academic lark for a month really help them?

With all this on my mind, life seemed to spark and crackle with an occasionally dangerous intensity. One evening at Elizabethtown, I was caught in a sudden downpour as I walked back from a restaurant downtown a few blocks away. Reaching the edge of the campus and staying under the thick canopy of trees there, I dashed toward a large gazebo that sat in a clearing at the bottom of the hill in front of the building where my guest room was. I ended up staying there, sheltered and dry, if a little windblown, for nearly two hours as vicious lightning tore through the air.

Watching the storm lash the treetops, I was reminded of the terrors and uncertainties I now associated with life in the outside world. In many ways, I had come to believe, during our years in the colony, that life in mainstream society carried many of the same hazards as this storm — the shocks and risks of sudden annihilation among them. At the same time, I really was not afraid. Having been an observer and curator of the wild storms that lashed eastern Arkansas in my childhood, this one offered nothing I hadn't encountered before. Being surrounded by all this unleashed energy was exciting and life-giving. It brought as many consolations as disruptions. By the time I had made my way back to the dormitory, I wasn't nearly as disconcerted anymore. If anything, I felt strangely enlivened.

When I returned to the community in early July, I was exhausted and even more conflicted about our coming departure. As the summer slipped away, this tension only increased. And when the September 11, 2001, terrorist attacks opened such an atmosphere of revenge and patriotism in the country, places like Starland began to seem like communities of resistance once again — places where people of faith and conviction were standing against the status quo of violence and military domination. For the Hutterites, this kind of social resistance had not been called for since at least the First World War, when the two Hutterite men died in an American military prison.

There seemed to be a point to being in the community, a sense that what all of us were doing there amounted to something beyond our own corporate enrichment. At times, it seemed we were actually presenting a witness for something – for peace, nonviolence, and resistance to the trends and corruptions of modern society. But were we? And was this reason enough to stay?

Still, as the fall deepened and harvest began, the time of year I had always enjoyed most in the colony, I began to seriously doubt what we were about to do. Sitting in the truck as the combines made their passes through the corn, I had a great deal of time to flail myself emotionally. Were we truly reneging on vows we had made before God and the community? Or was God showing us a way to move on with our lives, having taught us whatever it was we were supposed to learn here? If that were the case, the vows and their dispensation, either by God or the community, would take care of themselves. Surely, we told ourselves, God would not ask of us anything that would be harmful or wrong.

Some days, though, I felt determined and sure that leaving was the right, and in fact the only, path to follow. What made it hard was when some aspect of the community that we had truly loved in the beginning appeared before us again amid all the turmoil we saw the rest of the time – some sign of the openness, togetherness, and mutual concern that had drawn us there to begin with and that typified the ideals of Hutterian life.

I felt this way especially one night in November 2001, when the Northern Lights appeared above the colony. For me, the aurora borealis had always carried a strange and mystical energy that I could hardly describe to others, and usually didn't.

This night, around 10 p.m., someone announced on the intercom that the aurora had appeared in an especially spectacular form. Duann and I joined about two dozen other people who were watching the spectacle — one of the most intense and enduring displays I had ever seen. Most had gathered down by the shop on the section road where the open fields gave us a clear view of the entire sky.

Away from the streetlights in the yard, the darkness was complete except for the swirling dome of lights that seemed to coalesce just above our heads. This night the lights were like a broad circus tent, with an open ring of sky at their pinnacle, and seemed to turn slowly against the rotation of the Earth.

All around us, people were staring skyward, the women dark as ghostly crows in their plain dresses and black jackets. Watching the lights, and seeing our neighbors together like this, together and almost silent in the darkness, struck me with a sense of incisive beauty — a beauty that danced along the sharp edges of our life together, but in this case held and comforted us all. Standing there, watching everyone else looking at the sky and realizing that soon I would be turning my back on all this — on the life we had known amid these people and this place — I felt as if I were being slowly torn in half. It was a sensation of fear and displacement that would become almost constant during the weeks ahead.

Daily, I tried to convince myself that this decision was wrong, that moving to Kansas would be a disaster, even that God would have his retribution on us for breaking our vows to the community. Repeatedly I felt we had left everything about our former lives behind, only to grab it all back six years later. I found myself wandering the place day and night, trying to memorize it in its smallest detail, or to find some hidden sign that we were really supposed to stay. None appeared, of course, and our minds had been made up long before.

Even in the frigid December air, I would stand out by the county road and look back at the lights of the colony as the early darkness settled around us. During those weeks three blizzards blew through, reminding me that we could very well wind up moving in another snowstorm, just as we had when we arrived in Minnesota in 1995. All three storms, however, melted to the ground and the winter started out mild and relatively calm through Christmas.

As it turned out, we told David Vetter and David Jr. of our decision to leave the following January 6 — four years and a month after formally joining the community. We waited until the Christmas and New Year's holidays were over, not wanting to bring any upheaval to those celebrations. But with these behind us, and with my new job due to start January 17, we decided to move ahead. We told them we wanted to leave the following Friday and asked them to help us with the resources we would need to move.

Though David Vetter gently tried to dissuade us, he did not scold us or belittle our decision, as some might have done. If anything, he of all people had seemed to understand what we were doing in the colony in the first place, and why it would be so difficult for outsiders to join and thrive there. He also knew how difficult it would be to leave.

This discussion took place on a Sunday evening, and the next morning after breakfast, David Vetter gathered the baptized men in the church room and informed the rest of the community of our departure. Somehow, having this formality out of the way, and finally bringing our decision out into the open, gave us a sense of freedom and purpose we had not felt before. It did not make the transition any easier for us, however, in the long run.

Because we were leaving the community with the formal permission of the leaders, we technically were not severing our formal bond there. As David Vetter and I discussed, we essentially remained under a bond of obedience to the colony, meaning that if the community chose, we could be told to return. However, as David Vetter told me, he would never ask us to do anything that he knew we couldn't, or shouldn't, do.

Years later, the call to return has never come, nor will it. In this respect, our tie with the colony is severed, though we are not considered to be excommunicated. Instead, for what it's worth, we remain in a kind of vague and virtually unin-habited netherland, a place where we are neither members nor not-members. Strangely enough, this has been a place of comfort and peace so far, though also of uncertainty. While we remain free to do as we wish and join any other church we might choose, we never have, at least not yet. Somehow such a conclusive step would seem to erase that final connection we have retained, slight and inconsequential as it might seem to most.

Outwardly, in our daily lives, preserving and even nurtur-ing this bond means virtually nothing. But spiritually, in that corner of the soul where even the most weathered vows are always kept and cherished, this means almost everything – like the sometimes bitter remnants of a marriage, long-neglected perhaps, that one or both partners keep because they are just too holy to cast aside.

~

I drove away from Starland Colony at about 4 a.m. on January 11, 2002. It was dark and I was alone, driving the 1995 Chevy Tahoe SUV the colony decided to give us to start our new life. Though it had nearly 100,000 miles on it, like most well-used Hutterite vehicles it was in excellent shape and drove as if it were virtually new. At some point as I neared the Iowa border, I realized that I was following, but in reverse, the exact route we had driven when we had moved to the colony six years before. It all looked very familiar, as if nothing had changed in all that time, as if perhaps only a few days had passed since I last had been that way.

Duann and our children left later that morning on the Starland semi, which carried our belongings – our clothes and books, the children's toys, some of our furniture, essentially whatever we had chosen to take, along with about a week's worth of groceries Jake Decker had brought from the colony storehouse. Lisa Kleinsasser, Arnie and Ida's oldest daughter, had come over early and helped Duann get the children ready to leave. In a few years, she and her new husband, who would break tradition and move from Canada to his wife's colony, would move into our old house and make it their first home together.

David Jr.'s son, Kenneth Decker, drove Duann and the children all the way to Newton, Kansas, just north of Wichita, arriving at our new house, a place we had never seen before in a town I had never visited, at about eight in the evening.

In the weeks before I had dreaded the moment when I would actually leave the place for the last time. I had feared it would be too emotional and heartbreaking to even think about. But when the time actually came, I simply left our house, got behind the wheel, and drove away.

For all appearances, it looked as if I were only headed off to Minneapolis and would be back that night. I neither wept nor lingered for a final look, though I did wind up driving a circle through the yard when I found one of the exits blocked by a truck from another colony. That would be my last pass through the place where we had spent a large part of our lives, the only place that two of our children had ever known as home.

All the goodbyes had been said the night before, the last from David Vetter, whom I had watched from our door as he walked slowly back to his house in the darkness. Somehow I felt that our leaving especially disappointed him, a minister who had gone from being quite strict and traditional in his younger days to being open and progressive, welcoming to anyone who wanted to come along and try.

On the radio, as I turned off the section road and headed straight south, some Bartok piece was playing on an all-night classical music show out of Minneapolis. That's all I remember. It was shaping up to be a cold, cloudless morning, the fields and roads open and clear. Nothing seemed out of the ordinary at all.

But I was somewhere down at the crossroad a couple of miles away, turning toward Winthrop and then New Ulm, the defroster blasting against the windshield, when I realized that I was really no longer a Hutterite and never would be again. Even though I still wore the clothes of a Hutterite and drove a colony vehicle and carried a wad of $100 bills the community had given us to pay our rent and utilities for a few months, I was no longer a part of anything other than myself and my family.

All the way to Kansas, I felt neither sadness nor joy. Looking back, I felt nothing but some vague, deep longing for the faraway past. For some reason, if I could have gone back to my childhood in the South, even to my teenage years when I was virtually crippled and alone for four years except for Aurora Finn, I would have done it in an instant, if only so I could start all over.

chapter

NINETEEN

Of all the things we have encountered in our far-flung spiritual journey, it was the fields — the land itself, not some sense of ownership — that stood out most.

When it came time to renounce our common life in the colony, it was the sense of place, the sense of where we lived and who we were while we lived there, that presented the finest and most formidable blocks.

Those fields, that place of noctilucent snow and wind and gravel roads — and the city nearby, Minneapolis, with its museums and Somali bazaars inhabited by mysterious African Sufis — are what I continue to carry with me. Those open, fertile expanses of the Great Plains — those were the most haunting of all to leave behind. We were attached to these places by vows, by mystical locks and utterances that many people do not take very seriously anymore.

To our minds, we had attached ourselves not only to a church and a community but to God. And for me, God was most obviously present in the visible creation around us. I needed it — the smell and sight of it, the bitter slash of the wind opening and revealing every sense within me — and I feared I couldn't leave it behind for long.

The sad part was that no one — not one of our fellow communards — saw the same kind of blessing in our life together. Or if they did, they couldn't find the words to describe such a vulnerable state. They had become so used to this way of life that its uniqueness, its grace, no longer seemed to exist for them.

For many, the colony life had become a prison, or a palace — a self-reflecting culture instead of a place of spiritual fertility and ripeness. In large part, this pain and emptiness are why we eventually felt compelled — perhaps even called — to leave, though sometimes I still wish I could have made it otherwise. But farming, especially when the soil is planted with human lives, is full of disasters and always will be. Our humanity, and our proclivity to spark off of one another and cause pain, ensures this will be the case.

The year after we left the community, in January 2002, was the first time in quite a while that the occupation on my tax return would not read "farmer." Of all the transitions we have made, the occupational one may be the most significant. Not that I was much of a farmer.

But farming was what I enjoyed the most — in part because I got to go outside to do it, and because I enjoyed the dust and rattle of the cornstalks and the cool October breezes and the blue-black skies of late afternoon and evening when we went out harvesting. I think of this time now as if it were a lifetime ago, and I nearly weep. I always considered farming to be a great blessing, a vocation of undeserved holiness.

Sitting there, waiting in the truck for the combine to make another pass, watching as the corn piles up in the hopper and overflows, I felt as close as I ever did to the true and meaningful presence of God. It was silent and unwordable, and despite the din of our machines, I really heard nothing but the wind, which is the passing of the year, and the dry flutter of the swaying stalks stiffening, rasping, now receding as the breeze died down for a moment.

To the Hutterites, the farming life is a form of stationary pilgrimage, a journey to nowhere in particular but a journey nonetheless. It is a journey of the soul but also one that echoes the centuries of flight and persecution the Hutterites' forebears endured. As with most pilgrims, the strongest links are not forged with other people, the strangers and passersby in the towns around, but with the sacred land along the way.

Each fall, when we had completed the year's harvest, we had an *abschinka*, a harvest celebration that came, along with everything else, from Russia — like the *Hutterisch* word for strawberries or the polka dots on the women's scarves.

At that gathering, which we usually held on Thanksgiving, as much from convenience as from any symbolic meaning the day might have had in the world, the minister would read from Psalm 126.

This psalm is about harvesting God's gifts, in one sense, but it is also a song of pilgrimage, of exiles returning from a long sojourn — very appropriate for the Hutterites. Sometimes when I was alone in the truck out in the field as we harvested, I would stand amid the stalks and recite the psalms. It seemed natural and it filled my heart with the most profound joy.

When the lord restored the fortunes of Zion,
it was like a dream.
Then our mouth was filled with laughter,
and our tongue with shouts of joy;
then it was said among the nations,
"The lord has done great things for them."
The lord has done great things for us, and we rejoiced.
Restore our fortunes, o lord,
as streams in the desert.
May those who sow in tears reap with shouts of joy.
Those who go out weeping,
bearing the seed for sowing,
shall come home with shouts of joy,
bringing in the sheaves.

To many people, a life like that led in a Hutterite colony — or a monastic community or, for that matter, any church that tends to set the tone for the lives of its members such as the Amish — is so inward-looking that it becomes pointless, without value, wasting its time and squandering the graces bestowed on it.

It is little more than sowing and reaping, and then sowing again after the long, inevitable winter. But others find infinite value in people who set themselves apart, endeavoring to follow a spiritual path and seek communion with God.

While I do value the lives led by many people in Hutterite colonies, I know from experience that such an isolated life poses many hazards, whether one is isolated with God or not. These hazards can easily and quickly turn a garden of grace and light into a contrarian ghetto of inversion and blindness.

So what is the relevance of such communities as the Hutterites build? How do we relate to them as fellow spiritual travelers? Such places are as relevant as we are willing to admit. Either we accept their values or we do not. Most people, and likely most Anabaptists, do not accept the values that Hutterites embody — either because of their strict communalism or their distant, insular, kin-centered separation from the world. However, these are not the main values to consider.

Instead, we should look at the possibility in such a life for meaningful prayer or as a form of living witness. Indeed, the life led by Hutterites and other Christian communal groups is largely one of witness — even of a penitential witness that can heal us of our many faults. Most Hutterites do not look at the inherent, spiritual merits of their life together, at least not beyond the outward demonstration of living with all things in common.

They have been living this way for so long, with so little freshening in their midst, that their style of life has become, in places, desperately stale and smothered by forms and fallacies.

The Hutterites know they desperately need a revival, or a return to their beginnings, when they gazed not at themselves so much as at Christ — when they were still communities of resistance, of an alternative, of a different way that meant something to more people; when they were a refuge that welcomed fellow travelers to the fold. God will bring this revival in his own way.

Still, there is something emblematic in Hutterite life, something that does not have a name. It is something of immense value, even if we cannot relate to it, a kind of love and regard for one another that surpasses what most people will ever experience. Some of us can see it, others cannot. And there it will have to rest.

Living in our community was something we had to get used to, and possibly we never did. Indeed, in Hutterland, exile was an obvious commodity that one could get too much of without realizing it.

Getting accustomed to not living such an exile anymore has driven me even more deeply into it, I'm afraid — but perhaps in a good way. Very likely, that way was not to be found in the colony, where spiritual fulfillment for outsiders is no longer a priority, having gone out of vogue hundreds of years ago. In today's Hutterian world, by no one's fault, there is no means to support or nourish people like us, and we couldn't invent it ourselves. No matter. We were earnest and so were they.

When I feel particularly lonely now, I put on my old Hutterite clothes again — the handmade shirts, the still-dusty barn coat — and the dim chill warms away. The other day, I found a few old soybeans in a pair of boots I used to wear. They still seemed to smell and taste of the thick, black earth where we lived. At night I dream of the razor-straight county road that passed a mile east of the colony. I dream of it as it appears at night, in snow, beneath ancient starlight and shimmering auroras.

Across the sleeping fields, crisscrossed by foxes, I see the lights of the houses and sense the lives I realize I am a part of and yet can never truly touch again, certainly not from such a distance. In a world filled with such barbarity as the many wars we insist on waging, and the sinful starvation we inflict on so many around the world even while we build more bombs to kill them with, I can only say that my spirit resides on a distant road, in a faraway place where I no longer live, under moonlight.

I left a large part of myself there, and I don't think I will ever get it back.

EPILOGUE

Since we left Starland Colony in 2002, a great deal has changed there, just as it has in our own milieu.

I am very grateful to my family — my lovely and tenacious wife, Duann, and our three children, Shelby, Lydia, and Aidan — who have their own stories to remember and tell about our life in the colony. When we first moved to Kansas, our children spoke with thick *Hutterisch* accents and their English had sort of a backward German syntax. "I like it not," Lydia would exclaim when something failed to earn her satisfaction. For some time, we would hear all three of them, playing among themselves, still speaking *Hutterisch*, though this, and their accents, soon faded. Today, no longer using the archaic Hutterite High German, they claim little memory of their second or third languages, though *Hutterisch* has a way of reasserting itself. All of us still use occasional expressions we acquired, and once in awhile, I still forget the English words for certain objects, while remembering the *Hutterisch*.

Of us all, Duann probably made the greatest sacrifice in moving to Starland, where not only her education but her status as a woman relegated her in ways she had not experienced before. As a male, I really knew very little of the shared life of women in the colony, which was a close-knit society all its own. For Duann and the other women in the colony to have learned to accept one another could not have been easy, or entirely possible.

Thanks as well to all of the residents of Starland Hutterian Brethren, who did their best to share their lives with us from December 1995 to January 2002. Since we left Starland, several families and individuals we lived with have departed and started new lives in the surrounding area, or in other states. Though this is tragic in many ways for the community, it seems to be a trend among today's Hutterites, some of whom appear to experience a longing for the emphatic, mission-minded spirituality of long-ago Hutterianism. Others, as in many churches, have gravitated toward more mainstream evangelical groups. Meanwhile, a core group of families dedicated to keeping Starland vital seems to have emerged among those still living there.

I especially thank the Rev. David Decker Sr., whose support made our lives in the community possible and helped us assimilate into the deep, traditional strata of Hutterian life. Some time after our departure, David Vetter fell into ill health. On my subsequent visits to the colony, he had become increasingly frail, and eventually, was no longer able to walk on his own. Still, his strong constitution — bred on the Canadian prairie amid the bluster and difficulty of the life there — seemed to preserve him. Though he could no longer fulfill his role as colony pastor, he officially remained the senior minister, with Herman Wollman bearing the burden of leadership with David Jr., and the other witness brothers.

David Vetter died the evening of January 22, 2009, at the age of 86. It was my 45th birthday, and I had thought of David Vetter several times during the day. A few nights before I had a vivid dream of him, in which he was strong and well again. Though we had known his death was coming, I somehow thought he would always be there. It seems impossible that now he is not.

We also extend our best wishes to our friends and adoptive families in other Hutterite colonies in the United States and Canada, especially Baker Colony at MacGregor, Manitoba, and Crystal Spring Colony at Ste. Agathe, Manitoba. To Leo and Patricia McAdams, who joined Crystal Spring from the Bruderhof Communities during the upheavals of the early 1990s; Jim Evans, who joined Crystal Spring as a young man and later married and started a family; and Emil and Margaret Waldner of Baker Colony, who were faithful friends and supporters, especially to Duann — we still hold you closely in our hearts. Leo and Pat were our children's colony grandparents, and very close friends to Duann and me, having been newcomers themselves many years before — a status they still carry to some extent and always will.

I also thank my colleagues at *Mennonite Weekly Review* — Paul Schrag, Robert Schrag, Dana Neff, and Trudie Wiggers — where many of these ideas, and brief segments of this book, first appeared in various forms.

Other explorations of our life in community, during and since, have appeared in *Communities* magazine, *Mennonite*

Quarterly Review, Orion, The Catholic Worker, Media Ethics, Plain magazine, and several other publications. The ability and freedom to write about our time in the colony, even while we were still living there, was a valuable outlet for me, and helped me to draw sense from the contradictions we discovered there. This writing truly helped make me, as a doctor friend in Minneapolis put it, a "world citizen" who was not always comfortable with this status or responsibility.

My friend and mentor Miller Williams — acclaimed not only as a poet and teacher but as the father of singer-songwriter Lucinda Williams — has helped me as a writer in ways beyond number. In addition to his writing, he is one of the most skilled and intuitive editors I have known.

Ohio Amish farmer David Kline has inspired me as well. In the early 1990s, during my spiritual crisis, I came across his first book of farming and nature essays, *Great Possessions: An Amish Farmer's Journal.* When I read it, I thought this would be a good person to be friends with. Events soon brought us together.

To the late Shelby Foote: Thank you for giving me permission to be a writer, and for acquainting me with the attending hardships and sorrows.

And to Aurora Finn: Thank you for everything.

About the Author

Robert Rhodes is a former daily newspaper journalist who has worked on periodicals in Fayetteville, Arkansas, and Newton, Kansas. His poetry and nonfiction have appeared in numerous magazines and other publications. He lives in eastern Pennsylvania.